The Countryman Book of Village Trades and Crafts

The Countryman Book of Village Trades and Crafts

Edited by
ELIZABETH SEAGER

DAVID & CHARLES
Newton Abbot   London   North Pomfret (VT)   Vancouver

THE COUNTRYMAN GARDENING BOOK
THE COUNTRYMAN RESCUING THE PAST
THE COUNTRYMAN ANIMAL BOOK

(*frontispiece*) William Marshall throwing jugs at the Bernard Leach pottery (*Jeremy Grayson*)

(*jacket illustration*) Photographed in 1958, George Elliott of North Newington was then the only saddler still working in north Oxfordshire. (*John Saunders*)

British Library Cataloguing in Publication Data

The Countryman book of village trades and crafts.
  1. Handicraft – England – History – Addresses, essays,
  lectures 2. Country life – England – Addresses, essays,
  lectures 3. Great Britain – Industries – History –
  Addresses, essays, lectures
  I. Seager, Elizabeth
  338.4'7'68   HC256

ISBN 0–7153–7493–1

Library of Congress Catalog Card Number: 77–91719

Printed in Great Britain
by Biddles Limited, Guildford, Surrey.
for David & Charles (Publishers) Limited
Brunel House   Newton Abbot   Devon

Published in the United States of America
by David & Charles Inc
North Pomfret   Vermont 05053   USA

Published in Canada
by Douglas David & Charles Limited
1875 Welch Street   North Vancouver   BC

Contents

Foreword

The village shop up the lane from my first married home was a thriving, old-fashioned general store, somewhat cramped, rather gloomy inside, but full of a wonderful variety of merchandise, from potatoes, paraffin and pickles to beans, butter and brass polish. Behind the worn, wooden counter, wellington boots hung in pairs above sacks of onions and carrots, and hanks of knitting wool lent their soft texture and a dozen different colours to the intricate pattern of the closely-packed shelves where mousetraps and mops sat side by side with bacon and Bath Olivers.

The shop, far more than the parish church, was the centre of village life. The men might exchange their gossip over an evening pint at the local, but for the women the shop was the place to discover who had been born, or wed, who was dying or dead, and while the parish council settled official affairs monthly in the schoolroom, the villagers themselves set their own little world to rights daily in the shop.

Times change, and the old shop entered the swinging sixties with a flourish of Formica, frozen foods and fluorescent lighting. Knitting wools went out in a grand clearance sale at 6d an ounce and in came canned ravioli along with disposable nappies and fruit-flavoured yoghourt. The old wooden floorboards disappeared under a sea of shining vinyl, an adding machine appeared on the sleek new counter, and a pile of wire baskets near the door completed the transformation.

Less than ten years, however, were left for the villagers to enjoy this modern emporium, for on the owner's retirement his son swopped bacon and biscuits for a nice line in bygones and a new sign board announcing Country Antiques. Today in his windows, copper kettles, brass trivets, oil lamps and pewter candlesticks gleam invitingly for the tourists, while the locals have to travel into town for the practical necessities of life which, a few years ago, they would have found in their own village community.

Some village tradesmen keep a shop and deliver their wares to nearby customers – on the island of Sark delivery is likely to be by bicycle. (*Carel Toms*) Some provide a service: many, like this gardener photographed at about the turn of the century, devoted their whole lives to their trade. (*M. Littledale*)

Until the early years of this century most villages were largely self-supporting, and the inhabitants of almost any small rural settlement could go, as they had done for hundreds of years, round the corner, down the lane or up-along to their own baker, butcher, cobbler, draper, blacksmith, wheelwright, miller, dairy-man, dressmaker, thatcher, builder-cum-gravedigger and half a dozen more besides.

Often the village provided work for all, with each trade and craft employing several apprentices – a very different picture from the present decade when so few apprenticeships exist in the United Kingdom that the Craft Guilds in France, offering free training and hostel accommodation, are beginning to attract young people from Britain to be apprentice stonemasons and black-smiths.

Various factors contributed to the decline of rural self-suffi-ciency, amongst them the arrival in the 1930s of cheap transport; the upsurge of mass production in a variety of industries, which led to the death of many local crafts; and the replacement of the horse by the internal combustion engine. Sadly, the changing pattern that resulted in higher living standards and less insularity, also robbed village life of the warmth and vitality that springs from the casual day-to-day contacts of a small community whose members are dependent on each other, a characteristic that no amount of organised community activity can ever entirely replace.

For fifty years *The Countryman* has presented a realistic, pungent, often humorous picture of British rural life, and the following selection from its pages is intended not as a mere trip down memory lane but as a comment on the changing pattern of country trades and crafts, particularly those of the villages. The word 'tradesman' is used here in its traditional and widest sense to describe not only a shopkeeper, as in modern usage, but craftsman and artisan too.

Some of the chosen articles present a detailed picture of the technicalities of a particular craft, others describe the delightful eccentricities of village tradesmen, or reflect on changing times and methods – but nearly all convey that once-general pride in good workmanship, and satisfaction in a job well done, that is nowadays found only in the work of a dedicated few – men typified by Lancashire blacksmith Ron Carter, who in a recent

Others keep alive crafts in danger of being lost: a recent picture of Frank Tedham of East Sussex with a waggon he built during his 70 years as a wheelwright. (*Frank Tedham*)

radio talk described his craft as 'a lovely challenge – a wonderful struggle', and was cheerfully content to be 'always learning, never rich in money, but rich in other things'.

It seems particularly appropriate that this book should have been compiled in a small stone-built cottage under a thatched roof, at a desk which stands near the window where a previous occupant worked at the local cottage industry of gloving, glancing up now and then, as I do, at the flower-filled garden bounded by its neat drystone walls, beyond which wide fields slope steeply to the valley of the River Evenlode. Along the lane is a house where villagers once shopped for groceries and homemade lollipops; a nearby cottage was once the hamlet's forge, another an inn. New housing has replaced the old cottages beside the slaughterhouse and butcher's shop – empty since 1970 – and the quarries that once provided stone for some of the great buildings of Oxford have long since become a leafy playground for local children.

A community of commuters, we are typical of rural hamlets throughout the country and luckier than some, for we still have a tiny post office-cum-general store; and though the centuries-old country trades are in decline, they have not wholly vanished from our midst. Up the lane a neighbour is making a splendid job of erecting a drystone garden wall in the traditional manner illustrated here on page 91, and soon we hope (bearing in mind Joyce Ward's cautionary tale on page 67) to have the pleasure of watching the thatcher at work on a new ridge for our own roof. Even though he does come from fifteen miles away and not from our local community, it is encouraging to know that his son is following him 'up the ladder', thus ensuring the continuity of a traditional trade for another generation.

This anthology was originally conceived by loyal *Countryman* reader, Gordon Edwards, who had worked out the first synopsis when he so tragically died in the garden to which he was devoted.

Elizabeth Seager

Over The Counter

The Rise and Fall of the Village Shop   by Pamela Horn

In recent years the village shop has been gradually disappearing, under pressure of competition from High Street supermarkets and department stores; for despite the infrequent rural bus services, most villagers are able to fit in a visit to a town at least once a week to make their major purchases. In the nineteenth century things were very different. In those days visiting a town meant for many, either a walk of seven or eight miles, or else booking a place on a slow-moving carrier's cart which would probably take all day to travel there and back.

In such circumstances the village store prospered. At Haddenham in Buckinghamshire, for example, Walter Rose recalled that in the 1870s and 1880s 'the whole village' would converge on the 'Beehive' general shop, 'and it would be difficult to mention a need that it did not supply.' The shelves were stacked with canisters of tea, hogsheads of moist sugar, sides of bacon, cheese, butter and a whole range of other foodstuffs. There was also a section devoted to drapery and 'general' items, including bales of cloth, rolls of linoleum, ironmongery, candles, and paraffin oil for the lamps. Much earlier in the century Miss Mitford had similar memories of the shop in her small Berkshire village; it was as 'multifarious as a bazaar; a repository for bread, shoes, tea, cheese, tape, ribands, and bacon'. In many parishes there would also be a butcher, a baker, a tailor and a boot and shoe-maker – as at Wiggington, Oxfordshire, where in the early 1850s there were two boot and shoemakers, a baker and a general shopkeeper to serve a population of around three hundred people. At Stratton Audley in the same county, two bakers, a butcher and a general shopkeeper catered for the needs of a similar community. A brief examination of Victorian trade directories will confirm that these are typical of many thousands of parishes that could be quoted.

Yet it was not until the later seventeenth century that the

The market stall (*Brian Walker*)

village shop became a normal appendage of rural life: before this consumers had relied on bulk purchases from itinerant packmen or from local fairs and markets. Both then and later, vegetables were grown in the garden, many families raised their own pig or chickens, and the few items of furniture or ironware used would be home-made or else purchased direct from the village carpenter or blacksmith. Indeed, most of the earliest country shopkeepers regarded retailing merely as a sideline, to be combined with a craft or with farming or with keeping an inn. Not until the eighteenth and nineteenth centuries did the general shopkeeper become a familiar figure in his own right, and his advent was still sufficiently recent for William Cobbett to denounce him in no uncertain terms in the early nineteenth century. '*Shops* have devoured *markets and fairs*,' he wrote bitterly. 'Shop-keeping merely as shop-keeping is injurious to any community. The shop must be paid for; the shop-keeper must be kept; and one must be paid for and the other must be kept by the consumer of the produce. When fairs were frequent, shops were not needed. The shop hides from both producer and consumer the real state of things.'

Nevertheless even in Victorian times by no means all parishes enjoyed the convenience of a village shop. As late as the 1890s

Mapledurham in south Oxfordshire was without a store to serve its population of over 400 people; presumably they had to walk the four miles into Reading to make major purchases, or else place orders with the carrier to execute on their behalf. Likewise Harpsden, about two miles from Henley in the same county, was without a shop for a community of over 200. In all, around one in six of Oxfordshire's 230 or so rural parishes lacked a village store. In more sparsely populated areas of the country, like the sheep-raising district of Glendale in Northumberland, the position was still worse. It was even said here in the 1890s that the population was so scattered that there was a shortage of public houses! The inhabitants had to rely upon travelling carts sent out from nearby small towns, like Wooler, and upon the activities of hawkers and pedlars to satisfy their needs. It is perhaps not surprising that at the 1871 Census Wooler had no less than ten hawkers among its population of just over one thousand people – at a time when the national total for hawkers and pedlars was around 45,000.

The packman, therefore, provided a welcome substitute for a shop in districts where the population was too small to support one. Along with his ribbons and lengths of cloth, his garden tools, needles and cooking pans, he brought with him a welcome breath of the outside world. In the small parish of Filkins in Oxfordshire, George Swinford remembered how people looked forward every year during the 1880s and 1890s to the visits of a man named Burrows, who used to spend about a month in the village each spring and autumn:

He was agent for the cutlers named Brades from Sheffield. He had a large covered wagon where he kept his cutlery, and every morning he would be off on his wagon and two large black horses round the countryside, selling his wares to the farmers. In the evening he would lay his goods on the village green for the villagers to come and buy a pocket knife, a hoe, a billhook or some other tool they needed. His tools were known as good tools, and if we boys had one of Burrows' pocket knives, we thought a lot of it.

The village shop (*Brian Walker*)

When he first arrived 'his ware was spread out near the Lamb (public house) and we boys received a few coppers for going round the village with a bell, and telling them that Mr Burrows had come again. He seemed to do a good trade. If you did get a bad tool he would exchange it for a new one, next time he came.'

Still earlier in the century Filkins had been visited by a salt merchant named John Cobbett, from Lechlade in Gloucestershire, who 'used to bring salt round to the villages for sale in a small cart drawn by a team of dogs.' At a time when salt was widely used as a preservative his visits were important. He would arrive at about mid-day and stop at one of the public-houses for a meal, meanwhile letting his dogs run wild round the village to pick up a few scraps of food where they could. When Mr Cobbett was ready to resume his travels he would blow on a horn, and 'his dogs came back to him; he harnessed them up and was soon on his way again.' This use of dogs as draught animals became illegal in 1854.

Clearly such travelling salesmen played a vital part in the distribution of consumer goods at a time when shops were still relatively few and far between. But by the end of Victoria's reign their significance was already dwindling, as the increase in the number of shops and, more importantly, the availability of cheap bicycles helped to make their services redundant. For when people had the choice they preferred to do their shopping in larger centres, where prices were lower and goods more varied. Later the same two factors were to strike a blow at the village store itself. This latter trend was reinforced by the policy of some smaller shopkeepers of buying at least part of their stock in tiny quantities from one of their larger town rivals, and then re-selling the goods in their own establishments at a higher price.

But perhaps one of the most worrying problems for small shopkeepers has always been the bad debt. In Victorian times it was common for farm workers to settle outstanding bills at harvest time, but not all of them were able to wipe off their arrears, and in these circumstances a barter system might be adopted if the shopkeeper were agreeable. The records of a village shop in Devon reveal, for example, that a smallholder who owed the substantial sum of £9 10s in September 1895 managed to reduce

Then and Now by Brian Walker

'Far from the madding crowd's ignoble strife . . .'

Spring 1977

the debt a little by selling his entire potato crop to his creditor. Another man in a similar plight sold fowls, ducks and turkeys, bushels of oats, bundles of straw and most of his potatoes in a desperate attempt to solve his difficulties. One feels that such a solution would hardly be relished by most of today's rural shop-keepers – or at least such of them as are managing to survive.

As for consumers, in communities where village stores have already disappeared it will be but small comfort to reflect that they are coming face to face with retailing problems similar to those which once afflicted their Tudor and Stuart predecessors. Perhaps they too will have to find a solution for their difficulties in an old-fashioned mixture of self-help and buying in bulk.

Spring 1976

J. Drew and Son   by Jane Garner

Dark and poky, smelling of cheese and apples, string and pepper-mint, meal and dog biscuits, and on Mondays, Wednesdays and Fridays having an all-pervading odour of fresh-baked bread – this was the village shop. You entered it through a little, rickety door, hearing the clang of a small, tinny bell, wobbling on a rusty wire. You stumbled down three dusty steps, half blinded by the gloom after the bright daylight. After knocking your head against strings of onions and cannoning into a pile of ancient, empty jam-jars, you found yourself opposite a small, worm-eaten counter, worn shiny with the passage of many years. From behind this issued the shop-keeper. He was small and tremulous, with a benign face that reminded you of a last-Christmas walnut that had turned up round about November in one of the dining-room drawers. Sparse white hair, like the first powdering of snow, grew round this face which was set off by a pair of piercing eyes. In a voice that sounded like the swan-song of a superannuated concertina he asked you what you wanted.

The shop felt like a well. The small bow-window was just about on a level with your shoulder – a queer little window, filled with green, misty, bubbly panes of glass, each with a twisted knot of darker glass in the middle of it. As if this was not enough to exclude the trespassing light, the window was still further blocked with piles of apples and bottles of those old-fashioned sweets (aniseed balls, brandy balls and lollipops) seldom seen now. The counter was piled with things. A small ginger kitten lay curled up asleep in an open sack of sharps (middlings), and another, a black one, squirmed over your feet in pursuit of some elusive, fluttering shavings on the floor. A small fire, the flames of which seemed to leap perilously near a hank of dry raffia, threw a pleasant, mellow light. The orange glow enriched the dark, black-brown beams, winked and flickered on the green, white and brown glass bottles and made the swinging Spanish onions look like burnished gold. The whole scene was reduplicated in three witch-balls, respectively red, green and yellow, which hung from the low, sagging ceiling.

Through the open door behind the counter you got a view of the living room. There was a fire burning in the grate surrounded by cool-looking blue-and-white Dutch tiles, the armchairs covered in a dainty fading chintz. Before the fire, a tortoiseshell cat on her knees, sat an old lady. Her cheeks were rosy as a late autumn apple and her white hair rippled over her head as she bent over her knitting. A bracket clock ticked slowly and solemnly from between two vases of dried lavender on the mantelpiece.

You left the shop with your bag of bull's-eyes and looked back to see the small scrawled notice, 'J. Drew and Son, Licensed to sell tobacco'. That notice had been put up years ago, in happier days, for no boy had been seen behind the counter for more than twenty years.

Autumn 1951

Staff of Two   by Vivian Ellis

Nearly every townsman's ultimate dream is to retire into rustic seclusion and run a village store. The reality is somewhat different from the dream, especially when the store includes a Post Office and the owners of the store are also the entire Post Office staff.

(My last sentence is inspired by envy. One of my ambitions has always been to be a Post Office counter hand, not only on account of the generous take-home pay, but for the pleasure I would derive from putting up a pretty little card inscribed 'Closed' as soon as I spotted a sizeable queue about to form.)

Our village post office at Allerford in Somerset opens when the store opens and closes when the store closes, and while the owners are having their lunch. Moreover, this rural branch of the GPO (or whatever it is now called) has the advantage of being scheduled for preservation as an ancient building. It has an iron-studded wooden door, two square and two rounded chimneys in local stone, and an unrivalled bush telegraph system (in addition to the usual one) that has been going since the day of Miss Mitford. Not by the present staff – as quiet a couple as you would ever meet – but that old country saying 'Standing gossips stay longest' still applies. I remember listening to one lady's life story while patiently awaiting my turn at a village post office in Wiltshire.

There are, however, some delightful compensations. At what other branch, for instance, would customers find the lady behind the grille willing to assist them in the intricate business of filling in their Pensions, Road Tax, Registered or Recorded Delivery forms, especially so attractive and obliging a one as Mrs Howard? Some members of the what-do-you-do-in-the-country brigade might retort that she has more spare time. But a twelve hour day – three of them behind closed doors clearing up the shop – plus half an hour's addition on behalf of the GPO by her husband 'who has a head for figures' – does not leave a lot of free time.

Timothy and May Howard are a married couple in their mid-thirties. They have two children, Kim, aged twelve, and Stephen, aged seven. Asked whether they would like to see their children take over the shop, the parents thought they should first be given a chance to see a bit of the outside world. Kim would like to be a school teacher, which marks a great change from older genera-tions of village school children, some of whom were terrified of their teachers. She also plays the recorder. Stephen wants to be a cricketer like his Dad when he grows up, but at seven he has still plenty of time to switch to football, being one of Tottenham Hotspurs' youngest supporters. The store's half-day closing is on Saturday afternoons, so that he and Dad can watch their favourite sports on the television. In addition to Kim and Stephen, the family consists of two white cats, Twinkle and Billy, and a golden labrador they christened Sandy. In our village, pet foods are big sellers.

The moment you meet the Howards you realise they are 'all right'. Born within a radius of a few miles, they know the village and the villagers are their friends. Tim Howard and Terry Jones who is slightly younger once combined playing at the local cricket match with creating a world record at an egg-throwing competition at a neighbouring garden fête one Saturday afternoon. (Presumably the sporting events on television went unheeded on that occasion.) I have watched them throw an egg and catch it, without breaking it, at a distance of seventy-two yards which, without wasting a number of eggs, is quite a feat.

Timothy Howard had been a policeman, when he won a number of cricket and running cups. These stood him in good stead when he retired after five years to run the shop and found the local youth club. He has actually taught them to walk, seemingly a lost form of exercise among the young.

Traffic here has always been a problem, from the days of pony and trap. Nowadays there is scarcely room for two cars to pass in the narrow winding lane outside. Consequently custom is mostly local and varies little with the seasons. Recently, a car park has been built so that summer visitors who can manage to walk one hundred yards and prefer self-catering (greatly on the increase) can make their own purchases, buy and stamp their own picture postcards and post them on the premises. Many have offered to buy the business as well but the Howards are not selling. They like the life and the locals like them, from the village school-children to the oldest inhabitants.

Their oldest customer, Mrs Nock, is ninety and Mrs Baker, aged eighty-five, thinks nothing of trudging two miles each way from her home and back to do her shopping. Passing motor coaches —when able to pass – call the store the village supermarket (giggles) but how many supermarkets can give their customers personal service? This includes that excellent substitute for trading stamps, conversation. Of course there is the inevitable awkward customer, but the Howards pay little heed to sarcasm. As for those much advertised 'This week's Bargains', any tax cuts are passed on almost as quickly and with far less ballyhoo.

What supermarket, may I venture to ask, can lay its hands within seconds on such a diverse variety of items as paraffin, pre-packed coal, pet foods, fresh clotted cream and free-range eggs, a variety of soft drinks, tights and paper-backs (we are nothing if not swinging), cigarettes (bad for health and profit margins), tinselled greeting cards for the nostalgic and trays made by the mentally handicapped for the charitable? That is not all. Failing a goodly selection of cough mixtures, indigestion tablets and headache pills, May Howard will ring up the local doctor, while her husband is handy at mending a blown fuse. They can offer me a bag of sultanas for my pet robin, who is fed to the beak with an unrestricted diet of cheese.

The Howards, however, have moved placidly with the times, taking to decimal coinage as ducks to water, thoughtfully placing a huge conversion table on the wall for the uneducated such as myself. When they took over the store, neither had any previous experience in running one. They began by making improvements, not all immediately appreciated, for few villages care for innovations. For instance, the frozen foods started slowly enough, but now there is a craze for fish fingers, besides frozen vegetables in winter. In summer, we each grow our own and win prizes at our local flower show. At least, I do. During the hot spells the deep freeze is a boon for all, especially the children who like iced lollies. In winter they revert to their staple diet of chocolate bars and gob stoppers.

When they first arrived, the Howards reorganised the whole of the inside of the store themselves, working round the clock one Easter weekend. The outside (bereft, nowadays, of its thatched roof) is kept in order by their landlords – and mine – the National Trust. A small letter box is let into the wall and a large pair of shutters fold over the one leaded window. When the shutters are about to be closed there is a last-minute rush of visitors to buy. We locals know better. When the store closes, it closes. But behind those shutters, we all realise that the Howards are as busy as the bees in their garden in the old blacksmith's yard, getting themselves organised for yet another demanding day.

Autumn 1973

Andrew the Vanman by T. J. Morrison

Perhaps because the days of past youth are always golden I cannot remember Andrew the vanman ever arriving in the rain. The clachan where I stayed, and which he served, was a scattering of whitewashed thatched crofts on the northern shore of one of the larger Highland lochs. It shared a church – impartially set halfway – with a collection of crofts three miles farther up the loch. Andrew's headquarters were the post office-cum-general store of the neighbouring clachan. Though he was undisputed master of the road, the shop itself was ruled over by two elderly spinster sisters with gentle voices which emanated from lips the colour of blaeberries. Andrew came to us twice a week, and his stock ranged from Daisy headache powders and lisle thread stockings to black striped balls and shag tobacco. If word were sent to him, however, or an advance order given at a previous visit, he would deliver a bolt of tweed for a suit or even a young live pig.

Every cottage sent a representative to do business with Andrew, and all forgathered on the bridge over the burn fully a quarter of an hour before he was due. The older folk bartered local news, the children played and the young people exchanged those long shy silences which inevitably seemed to initiate courtship in those days. I was entrusted to represent the croft where, each year, I spent those gloriously long sunlit summer holidays which, then at least, were every Scots schoolboy's heritage. Like the others, I carried a pillow-slip for the provisions. It was long before detergent manufacturers waged war, but the pillow-slips were of uniform whiteness and they smelt of bog-myrtle.

Andrew arrived promptly, his lean face shining and pink as though freshly scrubbed; and while he let down the tailboard, courtesies were exchanged. We presented ourselves to him strictly in the order of our arrival, with the notable exception of Maisie. Nearly eighty, she invariably arrived after Andrew, muttering to herself, and he by tacit agreement would suspend business with anyone else to deal with her. She lived on her own close to the loch. Each morning her cow was driven to the hill by the lad who acted as herd for the community and he returned it to her for milking in the evening. Neighbours cultivated her potato patch and the pocket-handkerchief field of corn which helped to sustain her score of hens. She was a suspicious, secretive old woman, and in a less kindly society her many eccentricities would have caused her to be dubbed mad. But the Highlander, like the Turk, regarded those who were mentally afflicted as sacred, and consequently her neighbours would suffer none to persecute or mock her.

In dealings with Andrew money rarely changed hands. The commodities he brought us – tea, sugar, salt, currants, and luxuries of rice and bananas for crofters who took in city visitors – were exchanged for home-produced eggs, butter and cheese. To find how much he was owed or was in debt, he chalked up the calculations on the side of the van. Debts to him were usually carried forward to his next visit, while he redressed any deficit on his side by a poke of boiled sweets or a twist of tobacco. During these proceedings Sybil would crop the 'gypsies' grass' by the roadside and when she moved on to fresh pasturage Andrew, chalk in hand, would patiently follow with his entire clientele. After each transaction a swift rub of his sleeve was all that was needed to clean the slate for his next customer.

Only Maisie questioned the chalked-up calculations· translating half-pounds of tea and sugar into terms of butter and eggs, like sums set by the dominie in his less indulgent moods. She always insisted on a detailed explanation of each step of the transaction. This tiresome capriciousness was not explained till Maisie's death released the minister from his promise of secrecy. The old woman, he then revealed, had for years been as blind as a stone.

Autumn 1956

Postal Order for Two and Six   by Florence Hopper

The bell over the door jangled in my ears. My nose was assailed by a mixed odour of paraffin, onions and carbolic soap. Feet shuffled over worn bricks, and an old lady scarcely higher than the littered counter inquired as to my wants. Stepping up to the part of the counter which announced 'Stamps' and 'Postal Orders' I asked her if I could have a postal order for two and six.

'You'll hev ti wait a bit', the old lady informed me. 'T'postmaster is muckin' t'pigs out an' he'll need ti wesh his hands.' And away she shuffled to some back region to inform the postmaster that a customer was waiting.

I did wait for quite a while before I heard heavy grunts and the knocking off of a pair of wellingtons. Water splashed into a bowl, and there were more grunts and sighs; then a man crept noiselessly into the shop, drying a pair of beefy hands on a voluminous towel.

'Excuse me stockin'-feet,' he said, dumping the towel among the merchandise, 'but what could Ah be gettin' for you?'

I told him my wants and watched with some anxiety while he searched one pocket after another for his keys.

'Seems Ah've lost me keys', he said at last; 'bet owt Ah've dropped 'em in t'pig muck'.

Wellington boots were laboriously replaced, and the postmaster clumped away across the yard. I learnt that Omo washes whitest, that Bero rises highest, that Esso paraffin is best. A dead stupor seemed to settle on me, through which I heard the solemn tick of the long-case clock and the cackling of a hen by the back door. I had just decided to call it a day when the postmaster returned and triumphantly held aloft the keys liberally coated with pig manure.

'Shall just 'ev ti wesh 'em', he announced, but he was soon back with the outsize roller-towel which he threw this time into a tub of potatoes. All smiles and sotto-voce whistle he thrust the key into the lock and pulled open the drawer. A steamy hand riffled through a small batch of postal orders; there was a pause and you could have heard a pin drop.

'Now fancy that', he said. 'Ah doan't seem ti hev one for that amount.'

Summer 1957

Postmaster General   by a sub-postmaster

The telephone rings. 'Will you please give Horace Ball a message?' The postmaster is over seventy, the weather not good, and Horace lives some distance away. A slight reluctance must have crept into his reply, for an infuriated female voice rejoins, 'Well, since you are so snooty, I won't trust you with my message' – and the receiver at the other end goes back on the forks with a crash that must have taken years off its life. Another ring. A peremptory voice asks that someone in the village be informed that her husband will be coming down by the afternoon train tomorrow. The postmaster's mild suggestion that the telegraph system was invented for just such emergencies is met with an angry retort, and he does not get a civil word from the lady concerned during the rest of her stay in the village. A third ring. 'Please tell Trusty Samuels (his real name is much better but I dare not give it) to come and kill my pig first thing tomorrow.' This is a matter of real importance, so the message is delivered. A farmer sends a boy for several pounds' worth of insurance stamps and will send a cheque in a day or two. He does. A local preacher, aged eighty-four, asks for a registered envelope, and after ten minutes is only half convinced that he has to pay a penny extra for the envelope. The electricity supply people ring up. 'Do you know, please, whose supply is out of order and what is wrong with it?' The postmaster replies sarcastically that of course he knows everything, and he does happen to have the information. That is one of the charms of the job. We do know everything. Although I took on the job during the war only in order to save the office from being closed, I cannot make up my mind to drop it now. We sub-postmasters get first-hand information on all subjects, and the village conscience is in our keeping.

All the little extra duties, besides the usual routine work, were rewarded with the sum of seventeen shillings a week, for which I provided full-time attendance, two assistants for emergencies, and the use of a room with cleaning, lighting and heating. Now I get double that sum. Sub-postmasters are paid on a scale based on work done and our office is at the lowest point. In 1913, my sister received the sum of three shillings and sixpence a week for similar duties in another village. Yet she rose to heights which I have not been able to attain, for, when old-age pensioners turned up for the weekly five bob looking a bit seedy, it was her habit to restore them with biscuits and wine (this last must have been home-made). Money was worth more then, but the net income from the job must have been small. I have not got further than taking pensions to the old folks who cannot walk the mile or so from their homes.

Summer 1950

Saving the Post Office   by Jean Rowan

In our Highland village the sub-post office is known as 'the shop'. Overhead the pylons carry power away to the cities, but there is no electric light here owing to the cost of transformers; and within the shop's cosy brown varnished interior a paraffin lamp swings from the ceiling to light the wide counters and stone-flagged floor. In the old days the post-mistress operated the local telephone exchange and she was so often out with her hens that it was difficult to get a number in a hurry. Now there is an automatic exchange across the road. Because of the frequent blizzards it is often out of order in winter, but when the weather is open it is quick and efficient.

Her husband was postman until last year. He sorted the mail which came up on the van and set off on his rounds, pushing his bicycle over the hill tracks. During the winter storms he wore a woolly hat with ear-flaps, changed his bicycle for a shepherd's crook and was often up to his waist in snowdrifts. He was laid off after a threatened strike of post-office workers. The authorities decided they could raise money for higher wages by replacing the postmen in outlying districts with Land Rovers operated from main post offices. Our mail is now delivered an hour earlier in summer; but in winter, for weeks on end, places cut off by snowdrifts receive no mail at all, unless people choose to collect it themselves on foot. Owing to the new schedule outgoing letters do not arrive at the main post office in time to catch the midday bus. Saturday being half day, it is therefore impossible to send a letter away from the glen between Friday and Monday.

When the shiny red Land Rover arrived in the village the postman was out of work. He did odd gardening jobs to help out. He wore his old uniform, carrying his tools in his postman's bag, and finished his working day with the familiar words, "Well, I'll need to be getting on down the road'. When, in May, the gardens were all cultivated the only full-time job he could find was a heavy one with the Forestry Commission on a local estate. He is a small, slightly built man, not very robust; but if you ask his wife how he is she says, 'Fine' or 'No complaints'. There never are.

He is also the local mole-catcher, but this is a hobby for which he will accept no money – just toffees or ten cigarettes. It is difficult to press money on a northern Scot at any time if he knows you well. He likes to think he is able to help you for nothing. 'There's no charge'; 'I wasn't looking for money'; 'There's no hurry – any time' or 'I'll get it again' are the answers you get when your garden has been dug or your chimney swept; and it is up to you to defeat him at his own game. He is perfectly happy to be thanked with a nip of whisky or an ounce of tobacco or snuff; he finds the acceptance of money embarrassing, and it is part of his Highland courtesy to help you to forget it.

The sub-post office was threatened with closure at the same time as the postman lost his job. The authorities called a meeting in the town to discuss both matters, and the postmistress was invited, but no-one attended it. The Highlander knows he is inarticulate and incapable of presenting his case without help; he is also too proud to complain, and too much of a gentleman. Rather than argue he will give you the chair on which he is sitting. He dislikes arguing and allows his thoughts to drift down stream and over hills. 'Have you seen my plants?'; 'There's a salmon lying yonder at the bridge' or 'Look, John, there's a big fat thrush in the garden' is all the response you will get if you try to persuade him to take a stand against evictions or dismissals or the march of bureaucracy. This is not a polite way of asking you not to interfere. It springs from a genuine lack of self-interest and a deep sense of hopelessness that the world neither understands his plight nor is sufficiently interested to acquaint itself with the reasons for it. There is also a basic conviction, to which the Highlander now clings, that if you do not fight you cannot be defeated. He counts his spiritual integrity above the possession of worldly goods and finds lost causes sweeter than battling for selfish ends.

It would be unrealistic to suppose that the post office was kept open by the reflection in high places that the nearest one would then have been more than eight miles away. More likely it was saved by a shrewd Lowland streak in the members of our community. The village is on the fringe of the Highlands, and we inherit something from both worlds. When the test week arrived and records were taken, people came from far and wide with letters, parcels and telegrams, so that the takings were high and the post office was spared. Had it been otherwise our village would have been doomed. First the church is closed, then the post office, then the school; finally, like migrating birds, the last inhabitants dwindle away to join the flock, and the heather creeps down over the once-cultivated fields.

For the present then the crisis has been averted. Chocolates, biscuits, syrup and tea are still sold over the wide counters, and you can even post a letter in the box and write, 'No money. Please stamp. Pay tomorrow'. Once a week the postmistress continues to buy all the bread for the village, wraps it in newspaper and places it on a high shelf to be collected. If the carrier leaves a parcel of plants late on Saturday night, you can still be sure that the postmistress or her husband will bring them two miles on a Sunday rather than let them spoil. In our struggle for existence we have learnt to be good neighbours one with another, and soon perhaps the tide will turn and the glens will re-echo with voices. Already there is the promise of ski-tracks in the snow, and these may be the portents of greater things.

Autumn 1960

Frog Street grocer's   **Dr Harry Roberts**

Here is Mr Masters' portrait of Miss Wollcott of the grocer's shop in Frog Street. 'We used to arrive at Miss W's with a list of goods required. It was usual to find some half-dozen other customers sitting and waiting to be served. Miss W. was plump in person and slow in movement. The fact that several customers had been in the shop a good half-hour left her quite unperturbed. Miss W. would ask one of us to grind the coffee, which made an agreeable interval in the monotony. Village folk were most inquisitive about passing strangers. I can see Miss W., the horn scoop for ladling out sugar, etc., in her hand, stopping in her scooping when people passed in the street, waddling to the window and watching the strangers out of sight. Then she would turn round to ask customers: "Who's that? Do you know? Do you? Where be they going to now?" '

From 'More memories of a Somerset village in the Seventies'
Autumn 1945

The Universal Provider   by Harold Sumption

Ours was a red village: not in any political sense, though we were mostly dissenters and Liberals in the sturdily independent West Country way. The Devon earth was red, of course, and so were the cattle, for Friesians had not then invaded us; but it was the flames of hell that coloured the picture for a child half a century ago. They seemed to burn just below the surface, as though we lived on a volcano. Every Sunday one of the chapel guides would take us up for a peep into the crater. As carpenter and under-taker, Arthur Sheldon may have had a privileged view of the flames; he would quiver in the chapel pulpit as he warned us of the torments awaiting the unrepentant. I was never quite clear what is was we had to repent; most of our neighbours seemed to work too hard to have time for sin.

Henry Walters, our universal provider, grocer, baker, iron-monger and farm-implement supplier, was convinced that the last days were upon us, that there was little time left for repen-tance. Yet Henry was a happy man and could be heard singing Moody and Sankey in his garden and warehouse. He was humble about his business acumen, giving the Lord all credit for his constantly growing prosperity. Any of the local farmers would have trusted Henry with his life-savings, confident that he would return them when required with an honourable rate of interest. Quietly he gave help where it was needed, and always accom-panied that help with quotations from the Bible calculated to set the hearer on the straight and narrow path. They frequently did.

'Early to bed and early to rise' was a maxim deeply embedded in Henry's vigorous philosophy. Though his house-hold kept a maid, he prepared his own breakfast at 5.30 and then took a brisk walk before starting his business day at 7.30. Even the walk was put to good use; he would select suitable tracts and texts and pin them to stiles used by courting couples. One feels that their selection must have posed many interesting problems.

Henry's foresight was not limited to business matters. Antici-pating the medical reports by more than forty years, he believed that cigarettes were instruments of the devil; so the many hundreds sent to him by grateful companies at Christmas were consigned to the bonfire. With similar prescience he saw that cigars were different. He did not approve of them; but he sold those he received to a friend and gave the money to missionary work.

The Christianity preached in the village was too milk-and-water for Henry. He drove his Model-T Ford – later a Daimler – to a stricter variety of chapel some miles away, though he had qualms about Sunday motoring and would walk or take a lift with an unbeliever whenever possible. I once attended this chapel and was startled by the loud 'hallelujahs' and 'amens' with which the congregation punctuated the sermon. Henry's had the authority and assurance which I later came to associate with a principal shareholder's 'hear, hears' to a chairman's report.

Summer 1969

Town and Country   from an Oxfordshire reader's letter

The town grocer is a machine with a long-nosed steel face that grinds off the parings of your costly victuals and picks out the smallest and dingiest of his good things to make the balance almost touch the notch. In the country your grocer is your tried friend who shares in your public works, goes to personal inconvenience to supply you with a sudden 'corner' of needed bacon when unexpected friends arrive in their car for a week-end. Your country grocer expects to be asked and does contribute to your village outing or other fund with tea or sugar or other good things. Your butcher charges you a high price, but you may take your meat from his cart blindfold.

From an Oxfordshire reader's letter on the benefits of
country life
October 1929

At the Grocer's   by S.D.

A young man in a hurry strode from his car into our grocer's. 'Four gallons of petrol, please; I'm in rather a hurry', said he. 'Right, sir', replied Mr Trinder, and went on cutting ham. 'I'm in a great hurry', said the young man, as the flabby heap of sliced ham took the pointer nearer and nearer to the half-pound mark on the spring scales. 'Do you sit on that chair, sir', said Mr Trinder, indicating it with his two-pronged fork, 'and let your hurry cool off; can't you see as I'm serving a lady?' The ham cut, the grocer asked, as always, 'What'll be the next thing?' 'Well', I said, 'I wanted some potatoes, but you can get this gentleman his petrol if he's in a hurry.' 'Aye', said Mr Trinder, 'but do you want anything clean getting? You see, your potatoes'll mess up my hands as much as his petrol, an' if you want anything clean – well, I'd better get it before I start on the messy jobs.'

April 1937

Blackmail in a Country Shop   by Henry Hamilton

It was quite by accident that I came to know Biddy. My eldest brother used to run her errands every Saturday morning. When he fell ill with measles he asked me to deputise for him, on the strict understanding that he would receive half the remuneration. This, he assured me, would be ample.

Biddy kept an untidy huckster shop on the edge of the small village in Donegal where I was born and brought up. A home-made signboard projecting over the door described her as 'Grocer and Confectioner', and a card in the window informed the public that she was willing to perform such diverse tasks as dressmaking, jam-making and music-making; she played a melodeon at country dances. Nor did her accomplishments end there, for she 'measured' for heart-fever, had a cure for ringworm that was a family heirloom, and was expert at laying out corpses. At first she seemed reluctant to engage my services, possibly because her list of wants included a noggin of whisky and she was afraid a newcomer might form a wrong impression. In the end, after she had several times assured me that whisky was an infallible remedy for a peculiar illness to which her turkeys were susceptible, and from which they were suffering at that very moment, she decided to employ me for the day.

Biddy had a habit which endeared her to all her employees, and especially to my brother – a habit which, had I not felt bound to discourage it, must surely have brought her to the threshold of the workhouse. Instead of handing you a lump sum at the end of the day, she paid you after each errand an amount in proportion to the distance. To connive at such extravagance seemed to me sheer dishonesty, so I took it upon myself to point out to her the folly of the system. When my brother discovered what I had done, he would listen to no ethical explanation and took me to task in a manner too painful to recall, thereafter turning his attentions to more profitable pursuits. My concern for Biddy's financial welfare was not without ulterior motive. Secretly I hoped that, in deference to my remarkable business acumen, she would one day ask me to look after the shop in her absence.

Proudly referring to her little establishment as 'The Business', Biddy hoped that, conducted as it was on a strictly cash basis, it would go from strength to strength until she would have to take over the empty cottage next door. When I first made her acquaintance there were about a dozen shelves covered with red crêpe paper, a crudely constructed counter and a tea-chest in which she kept bread. In a corner near the door stood a barrel of salt herrings into which she would plunge her plump arm for 'one with a roe'. When she withdrew her arm from the brine it would be covered with silver scales to the elbow, but it never seemed to occur to her then to wash her hands before serving bread. The shop was separated from the kitchen by a partition almost entirely covered with cards of sedatives guaranteed to banish all manner of nervous ailments. Perishable commodities were stored in the kitchen on top of the dresser where she kept a little stack of withered St Brigid crosses.

Before long I reached a stage of friendship with Biddy that gave me the freedom of the whole shop. I could come and go as I pleased behind the counter – that wonderful dark region from which rose the mingled scents of aromatic-flavoured sweets, cloves, fresh bread and Lifebuoy soap. It was quite some time, however, before I learned that Biddy had a husband. He never appeared and she did not refer to him; but as my visits to the shop became more frequent I would occasionally see him sitting, shoeless, with his feet in the ashes in the kitchen. He wore coarse grey socks which had singed patches all over them, as if they had been splashed with iodine. Even in the house he wore an old army overcoat, unsuccessfully dyed blue, and what was once a white silk scarf tied in a tight glazed khaki knot at the throat. He was a small man with shifty eyes and a silent tongue. Sometimes he chewed tobacco which looked like a roll of dusty liquorice as it was fished out of his pocket.

Years later I heard the reason why Biddy's husband had withdrawn from the public eye. It seemed he had had a passionate interest in dogs, and this had led him to cross a sheepdog with a greyhound. For the first few months the litter had shown all the characteristics of their greyhound mother; then they began to develop a certain shagginess about the tail and a kind of distant docility in the eye which betrayed their paternity. Their owner was upset about this, for he had hoped to pass some of the puppies off as pure-bred greyhounds. As he looked at the melancholy mongrels with their clean pointed heads, long lean bodies and incongruous bushy tails he decided to clip off the offending hair, take liberties with the best greyhound blood in the land and compose an impressive pedigree for them. This he did and, unknown to Biddy, sold the most genuine-looking at a fair in the next town. Before long, however, the sheepdog strain began to reassert itself. Biddy had to refund the money, and her husband was so ashamed of himself that he began to live the life of a semi-recluse. So the story went.

In the shop a large china bowl decorated with garlands of red roses served for a till, and sometimes Biddy would let me count the coppers and small silver at closing time. This gave me a greater sense of responsibility and was, I felt sure, an important step towards the realisation of the ambition that obsessed me day and night. One day soon she would let me serve customers. Meanwhile, convinced that I had not much longer to wait, I began to familiarise myself with prices and learned to manipulate the scales. At home I practised wrapping up books and other articles. As I lay in bed, I used to think of what I would say to my first customer and decided that, when my opportunity came, I would top Biddy's abrupt 'What d'ye want?' with a polite 'What can I do for you?" – prefaced, of course, by some remark about the weather or, better still, an inquiry after the prospective purchaser's health. Such a courteous deferential approach could not fail to draw trade to the shop.

About this time the conversation lozenge was an important and attractive feature of the confectionery trade. A hard flat sweet on which was printed some amorous question or flattering endearment, it was much sought after by the country lads and lasses who came to the hiring fairs. It must have proved an indispensable medium of courtship to many a bashful gossoon, sparing his love-baffled tongue much embarrassment. Indeed, in that part of the country many successful romances were known to have been conducted by means of these ten-a-penny sweets. For hours I would sit behind Biddy's counter on a biscuit tin and pass the time by reading the tokens of tenderness and avowals of life-long devotion, and afterwards it was only by the greatest effort that I could keep my conversation free from all kinds of romantic utterances.

That winter there was a slight epidemic of flu and I found myself half hoping that Biddy would become temporarily indisposed, so that I could step into the breach; but I was the one to fall ill and had to stay in bed for a week, in constant fear that she would take on another messenger. This did not happen, and I was soon haunting her premises once more.

The summer holidays were drawing to a close when one morning my chance unexpectedly came. Old Mrs Delaney of the post office died suddenly, and Biddy was summoned to perform the business for which she was so widely famed. The news sent her into such a flutter of excitement that she hardly knew what she was doing. 'Keep yer eye to the shop for a minute', she commanded as, without waiting to remove her apron, she made off. Proudly I took my stand behind the counter and was immediately tormented by the thought that perhaps nobody would come in before Biddy returned. I was about to give up hope when Andy Molloy, a neighbour of mine and a serious rival in school, bounced into the shop. I knew he envied me my position of trust. 'Me ma wants a quarter pound o' tapioca', he said, and glared at me defiantly, as if he did not believe me capable of executing the order. I would show him.

Unfortunately Biddy kept these comestibles in large unlabelled jars and, whether it was due to my eagerness to display my ability at weighing or to a natural nervousness over my first sale I do not know, but I served my sceptical customer with barley instead of tapioca. If he noticed the error, he maliciously held his peace. Five minutes later he was back in the shop, dumped the bag on the counter and gave me a withering look. 'A fine shopkeeper you are that doesn't know the difference between barley and tapioca', he jeered. 'Me ma might 'a destroyed a whole pint o' milk.'

I knew for certain that my terrible mistake would be broadcast round the whole neighbourhood and would surely reach the ears of Biddy, with disastrous consequences. In panic I thrust a handful of sticky wine gums at my tormentor and thus delivered myself into the hands of an importunate blackmailer. He shared my shilling a week for the best part of a year.

Summer 1960

Twopence Coloured   by Meg Stevens

Emily Oldroyd's sweet-shop stood at the downhill end of the village square. It was so small and so exactly on the corner that it was nearly in the Bradford road. That would have been dreadful, because the Bradford road was black and gloomy and haunted by terrible old ladies in carpet slippers and red-haired Irishmen with only one leg; all the fiercest dogs in the village lived there. It was no place to suck mint humbugs. The square was different. Nice ordinary friendly people whom one knew lingered in it. They shook dusters out of bedroom windows and exchanged confidences in shop doorways. Small boys balanced themselves on one toe on the edge of the stone horse-trough in the middle, or hung upside down on the railings outside the Bull.

So it mattered a good deal that Emily Oldroyd's shop was in the square, even if the window-sill was on a level with one's feet, and the door buried away in a dark cave three steps below the street. Immediately behind the counter was the old lady's sitting-room, from the dim depths of which she rose slowly when the shop bell rang, folding her knitting and stuffing it into her apron pocket. Wonderful aprons she had, sprigged all over with the most outrageous blossoms: all her other garments were of no particular shape or colour. Sometimes she wore a mob cap, which never struck us as funny, though few women still wore them about the village.

On fine days she would often sit just behind her window-shelves, keeping watch on the village through a curtain of

'Her head would loom out from the liquorice fringe'

liquorice bootlaces. It was disconcerting when one's eye, wandering contemplatively along the rows of tall glass bottles, encountered among pink sugar fish and pear drops that of Emily Oldroyd herself, glaring out from the other side. If one lingered too long with nose pressed against the glass, her head would loom out from the liquorice fringe and shake itself so fiercely that the sausage curls on either side of her fat pale face threatened to come adrift. 'Y' either coom', she shouted, 'er go'. And if you had no pennies, you went.

Daring little boys had been known to linger and stick out their tongues at her over the intervening confectionery before they fled round the corner. She would come out then and stand in her carpet slippers three steps down, so that she appeared to be rising out of the pavement like a spirit conjured from infernal regions. She rarely reached the top step, for she was stout and short of breath; but she would stand there glaring until she was satisfied that law and order had been restored.

I cannot determine, on looking back, why we bought our sweets from Emily Oldroyd. We were so terrified of her and could have got them at the newsagent's higher up the village. But we gravitated towards her shop on Saturday mornings as if under a spell.

All was hushed and dim inside. The hysterical note of the door-bell went jangling round the dark rafters, disarranging the silence so rudely that we almost took to our heels there and then. We stood, round eyes level with the counter, talking in whispers; and if she did not appear at once we sometimes tiptoed away.

Yet the darkness and dimness were part of the spell. Over the counter we gazed at the fire which flickered in the great black range, half expecting it to reveal unspeakable horrors in dark corners. Overhead on the mantelpiece was the most amazing collection of ornaments, disposed on a fringed velvet cloth. Chief among them was a clock, supported by four brass mermaids, and a pair of china figures of William Shakespeare wearing rose-sprigged trunk hose and looking mildly surprised at finding him-self to be twins after all. The walls were shiny and yellow with the treacly appearance of fly-paper. The pictures looked as if they had been painted with the same substance a shade darker. In them writhed shapes of dragons and strange headless monsters which the pure light of day would doubtless have revealed as nothing more terrible than 'The Sisters' Evening Hymn' or 'The Sailor's Farewell'. A great ginger cat sat by the fender staring into the fire with narrowed eyes, or washing himself carefully. You might have supposed the bald patches in his fur to be the result of over-zealous cleanliness, save that he lacked half one ear and most of his tail. He was his mistress's only companion.

Emily Oldroyd seldom smiled. When she did, it froze the marrow in our bones. She stood there waiting for us to say what we wanted, showing all her teeth as if she were secretly reviewing sundry wicked confections brewed in the night from ingredients which included toads' legs and bats' wings. But the only ill effects we suffered from her merchandise were largely due to the unwisdom of childless uncles, who occasionally gave us sixpence to spend all at once.

Spring 1965

The Old Toffee-maker   by Marjorie Giles

Old Toffee Tipton, who lived down the road, would be what is now called an anti-hero. Certainly his virtues were of a negative kind; he did not drink, he did not smoke and he was a mild-mannered little man. His shortcomings were too vague to be called vices; in fact, to most people he was just an ordinary chap. To us, the local children, he was rather special.

I am writing of the time around the beginning of the First World War which, living in a small country town in Shropshire, hardly affected us except that the world seemed a brighter place when our fathers came home on leave.

Toffee Tipton sold sweets. Not only did he sell them, but he actually made them, in a tiny one-man factory in the garden behind his little cottage. I had two brothers and two sisters (I was the girl in the middle) and to us getting into that factory was to step into another world.

Toffee Tipton was about seventy, a lean, shortish figure with a nut-cracker face, no teeth, sharp blue eyes, and a very pink skin. He had a sparse beard and snow-white hair. He always wore overalls and a flat tweed cap pulled down over his eyes. I never did see him without that cap. He was always busy and always worried. His wife and grown-up daughter both strongly disapproved of everything about him; either of them had only to say 'Now, Father' in a warning tone to send him scuttling down the brick path to his sugary sanctuary, inside which they never set foot.

The factory was built of brick, and from the outside it looked rather like a chapel, with narrow deep-set arched windows and a wide wooden door. Inside it was warm with the glow of the fire and fragrant with the aroma of peppermint, almonds, chocolate, and all sorts of mouth-watering smells. A huge brick stove with a blackened iron top stood at one end and on it several large pans bubbled away merrily.

Above the long table in the middle of the room two or three oil lamps were suspended from the crossbeam. On the table bowls, tins, spoons, bottles, scales and weights were spread in fascinating disarray. Along the walls were shelves filled with large jars of sweets, tins of toffee, stacks of paper bags, bottles of flavouring, and on the floor sacks of sugar with their tops turned back lolled against each other.

The most enchanting thing in the whole place was a machine which, when Toffee Tipton turned a handle, set in motion four

The toffee factory (*Brian Walker*)

metal arms which, passing through a bowl of soft toffee, turned and twisted and stretched it over and over again until it was of the right texture. The old man would pull out a piece of toffee about six inches wide and a yard long, and cut it off with an enormous pair of scissors; then he put it in another machine – a cross between a mangle and a mincer – turned a handle, and a shower of caramels would fall into the bowl beneath.

If one of us had a penny or even a halfpenny to spend, we could all go in through the gate and down to the factory. Once inside, Toffee Tipton would let us stand by the door, watching, for as long as we liked, but if we forgot and crept nearer, he would be afraid of our being splashed with boiling sugar. Then he would shout 'You—you—you kids get outa here. I wunna have ye meithering me.'

Then he would push a handful of sweets into our fists and scowl, with a twinkle in his eye, 'Now get off with ye.' He never accepted our pennies.

On one never-to-be-forgotten occasion, when I was the only spectator, Toffee Tipton actually asked if I would like to oil the moulds for the sugar mice. I was delighted. There were two dozen moulds in trays of six, rather similar to mother's bun-tins. I had a little brush, and some olive oil in an old cup, and my job was to see that each mould was given a very thin coating of oil. Then Mr Tipton came and poured the shining, almost transparent syrup into each mould. As it cooled, it became hard and opaque and, when about half set, we poked string tails dipped in sugar syrup into each mouse. Later on, when they were turned out, Mr Tipton gave them pink cochineal eyes and noses. That was a great day.

We used to like watching the humbugs being made. Two slabs of soft, peppermint-flavoured toffee, one black, one white, were put together and worked by hand, folding and stretching over and over again, until the two intermingled in black and white stripes. The stripes got narrower and narrower with each folding until at last the toffee was ready to go through the cutting machine.

Sometimes, if the old man was not quick enough with the folding, the toffee would set hard, and then it would not go through the machine. Then it would be left in slabs, broken up with a toffee hammer, and sold in lumps. These lumps had very sharp corners but they lasted a long time, and so were very popular with us.

Often, of course, we did not have any money to spend. Then we did not dare pass Mrs Tipton's door; she was quite likely to pop out and demand evidence that we were bona-fide customers. We had a routine approach to this problem. We would gather together, and casually mention to mother that we were going to play in the old pig-sty at the bottom of the garden. Well, so we did, but not for long. Soon we would decide to 'go trailing.'

Although we girls knew that we should be scolded for such unlady-like activities, the temptation was strong, and more often than not we followed where the boys went, hoping we might get away without tearing our rather bulky clothing. My elder brother always went first, and he led us through a hole in the hedge, then on all fours past the currant bushes in the next-door garden, and into the hen-run. Very quietly, so as not to start the hens squawking, we climbed on top of the pen, over the wire and into the over-hanging branches of the apple tree behind the factory,

Toffee Tipton's loaded handcart (*Brian Walker*)

down on to the grass and finally, with great caution, round the corner of the fuel shed and in through the door, without falling foul of Mrs Tipton.

On Wednesdays and Saturdays Toffee Tipton used to get out his old handcart from the shed, dust it down, and load it up with his wares, adding a pair of shiny brass scales and weights, a selection of paper bags and an Oxo tin containing a shilling or two in coppers. Then he pushed it down to the market and set up his stall under the Butter Cross along with all the country folk who had brought in their farm produce.

Very attractive it looked with boxes and jars of humbugs, caramels, peardrops, turkish delight, pipes and boot-laces of liquorice, aniseed balls, treacle toffee, bull's eyes, gobstoppers, sugar-mice and sugar-pigs with curly string tails, and pretty little scented sweets in delicate colours of mauve, white, pink, green and yellow, which looked like little satin cushions. In those days you got a lot for a penny!

One Wednesday morning, just as Mr Tipton was setting up his stall, he saw the young squire coming along in his new motor-car; at that time still a novelty. The noise of the car frightened a pony being driven by a farmer; the pony reared and the farmer's wife was thrown out of the trap.

Toffee Tipton managed to catch her or she would have crashed into one of the stone pillars of the Butter Cross. Both he and the farmer's wife fell on the sharp cobblestones; she picked herself up and ran after her husband without a word of thanks to poor old Toffee, who himself was suffering from several cuts and bruises. His stall had been overturned by the plunging pony, and all his goods trampled into the ground; quite a heavy loss for him. However, he told my father some time later that when the old squire heard of the incident he made ample recompense.

After the war we moved to another part of the county, and later I heard that my old friend had died. Most of his sweets were priced at a penny for a quarter of a pound, so Toffee Tipton could never have made much money. He would have found the changing world difficult, and a modern public health officer would give his little factory short shrift, with its lack of fire precautions and unhygienic conditions. But I never heard of anyone taking harm from eating Toffee Tipton's sweets.

Summer 1971

Public Bakery   by Ronald English

My father and, before him, my grandfather, were family bakers. When I first saw the title printed on a thin paper bag in the shop I was somewhat perturbed, especially as, a few doors away, was a shop with the words 'Family Butcher' over the door. At the bottom of the paper bag it said 'Public Bakery'. These significant descriptions of the family business seemed incredible at the time, for although I was only ten years old I knew we did not bake families or go out into the public street to bake.

A public bakery is now a thing of the past, but forty or so years ago it was very important to people living in the small terrace houses in the back streets near our bakehouse. Of course, public bakeries go back much further than that. They are mentioned in at least two places in the Old Testament (Hosea vii. 4, and Jeremiah xxxvii. 21), there was one in most Roman towns, and in the thirteenth century bakers were required by law to permit a servant to enter the bakehouse in order to make and knead dough for his master's bread. Furthermore, 'respectable persons' – presumably the masters – were to be allowed to watch their bread being made.

No one ever came into our public bakery in order to make his master's bread, but there was a daily procession of people with meat, puddings and cakes to be baked in the ovens. The dishes were placed on a long board at the end of the bakehouse, and a small piece of greaseproof paper with the name of the owner and the time required was put on the top of each.

A stranger in the bakehouse might well wonder at the many instructions given by the customers. Mrs Briggs wanted her roast beef juicy, Mrs Wright preferred her meat 'sharp', and there was one lady who always asked for her cake to be 'toked' well. It was a good thing my father and his assistant knew what each customer meant, though sometimes it was a matter of making the best of a bad job. There were Mrs Middleton's cakes, for instance. In spite of advice she always mixed in far too much sugar. However the cake was baked it always rose, overflowed, and then sank. The piece of cake that got baked hard on the oven bottom was, Mrs Middleton said, the part her husband liked best.

There were three ovens, one above the other, in our bakehouse. The bottom one was small and used only for proofing buns and certain cakes. The others were like deep caverns, with heavy iron doors and polished steel hinges and handles. Beside each oven was a jointed gas bracket with a jet. When the bracket was extended and turned into the oven the small jet lengthened into a flame about eight inches long, lighting up the interior right to the back. In the tops of the main ovens were many pipes, close together, and running lengthwise. These contained the steam that heated the ovens, a feature that gave rise to the statement 'Model Steam Bakery', included in all our advertisements. Such ovens are, no doubt, still in use, but in the 1920s they appear to have been worth boasting about.

The top oven was kept at a lower temperature than the other, and was used for cakes and puddings requiring slow baking, and for meat after the roasting had been started in the middle oven. Public baking began at about eleven, after the bread had been taken out and stacked ready for delivery. Making and baking bread was the biggest job of the day. It was mixed early in the morning and left for some time in the dough trough while the yeast did its work. Then the dough was emptied on to a huge board on which it was cut, weighed and kneaded. The loaves were then placed in greased tins and covered with cloths for a further period of proofing before being slid into the oven on the largest peel we had. Peels, up to 10 ft long, were held in an overhead rack in the bakehouse. A peel is a long-handled, flat shovel, and the largest would take up to six half-quartern bread tins at a time.

After the bread came the buns, pastries and fancies, the public baking, and, in the afternoon, the best quality cakes together with trays of pork pies, haslets, chaps and faggots brought in by several butchers. As a boy I liked to be around when the chaps were taken from the oven. They were placed in dishes to cool, and invariably there were a few pieces of meat left sticking to the tin in which they had been cooked. These pieces were delicious with new bread.

During the periods of depression in the 1920s public baking increased considerably. Fuel was expensive, and people found it cheaper to manage without fires and to pay the penny for a roast or bake in our ovens. Most of the small houses had only an open fire and a side oven for cooking purposes, and landlords were reluctant to spend money replacing these small ranges when they became worn. Consequently, food was often ruined when smoke leaked into the oven or the flues failed to spread the heat evenly.

Another thing I remember about those lean years was the development of the 'stale cake' business. Many folk could not afford new cakes and pastries and sales dropped heavily. The family baker had to keep up the variety of foods for those who could pay for them, and it was uneconomical to reduce the quantities made. So, when an old man with white hair and a drooping moustache asked whether we had any stale cakes we let him have two or three for the price of one. It was not long before many former customers were back buying stale bread and cakes. A fruiterer a few shops away reported an increasing demand for specked oranges and apples, and butchers were selling more penny faggots than ever before.

It must have been about this time that we began to make

Nelson squares. These were heavy squares of cake with a layer of pastry on the top and bottom. The cake part consisted largely of unsold cake crumbled down and made into a new mixture with a little water and additional fruit. Although heavy, a Nelson square was quite palatable, and the demand for them remained long after the years of real depression.

I suppose we were called 'family bakers' because so many families ran up accounts with us. In good times the accounts were paid regularly, but during the years of high unemployment collecting debts was one of the biggest problems. Even so, we never put anyone into court, for that was the most certain way of losing customers.

Autumn 1972

Country Bread   by Evelyn Hardy

I have just watched the third baking for the day at our village bakehouse. The baker, whose father before him was village baker, is between seventy and eighty, and has been at it since five o'clock this morning together with 'the baker's man'.

At five, 'the baker's man' begins to fire the oven, or a pair of ovens if a double quantity of bread is needed. The smaller oven is called the sack oven, because it holds a sack of mixed flour, and the larger, the sack-and-a-half, which means that it holds 420lb or more. Into these caverns of brick, around which the walls of the house and the mill are built, bundles of furze are pitchforked. To light the fuel the baker has a little iron lamp of much the same shape as the lamps used in ancient Greece or Rome. The wick is steeped in animal fat, since no mineral oil must taint the bricks or make a noxious smell.

The bread which is to be baked is made in great wooden troughs, almost as old as the mill itself, four-sided, narrower at the base than at the top and standing on four braced legs. To a sack of flour the baker puts three and a half pounds of salt and ten to twelve ounces of yeast – in hot weather the yeast rises more quickly and less may be needed. When of a proper consistency, the dough is lifted on to flat boards laid across the tops of the troughs, where is hangs over the edges like a soft, spongy, recalcitrant fleece.

The baker in his white apron, and a white, frilly hat, which droops over his white hair like the petals of an inverted flower, takes his knife and hacks at the dough. With his left hand he flings a lump on the weighing machine, making up the odd ounces with a scrap from his right, and throws the lot to his assistant at the far end of the table.

'The baker's man' works quietly and deftly, kneading a couple of loaves at a time. With the heel of his hand he presses downwards into the dough, his wrist rising and falling as the fingers turn and recover it. A younger man than the baker, he has been working for more than forty years in the low-beamed, primitive room with its worn flagged floor, the doorway six inches higher than the floor, and the ceiling blackened by puffs from the ovens.

The two-tiered cottage loaves are weighed up in halves. The popular 'sandwich' loaves, which are to be baked in oblong tins, the baker says he 'can't abide; if I had to eat one I suppose I could, but there isn't the goodness in 'em that there is in t'others'. There are also the 'coburgs' – round, single loaves – the 'long toms' – twisted loaves nicknamed after the Boer War guns – and various loaves of special proportions baked for time-honoured customers.

By now the baker's daughter, dark, sturdy and smiling, has come in to help. She takes the tins from a tall stack and sets them ready for 'the baker's man'. He throws the kneaded dough in and she slides on the tin lids with their furled corners. In comes the grandson, too, and sticks the heads of the cottage loaves with a round, pronged implement, like a pin-cushion with long, protruding, spaced spikes.

'The baker's man' peers into the open oven, takes down a long-handled rake and draws out the grey, spent twigs and ashes from the oven floor into buckets, and carries them to a pile in the garden. This done, he takes the long handled 'scuffle', a pole from which is suspended a chain and three strong bags filled with rubble or bits of brick, and dips it into a bucket of clean water and scours the oven floor, until the sweat stands on his forehead.

The handles of the rake, scuffle and various 'peels' – which come into use at the end of the baking – are made of polished teak, ash or hazel. First into the oven go the loaves in tins and then, in neat rows, the white, naked, puffy ones. 'The baker's man' places them deftly with his peel, hurrying so that the first lot may not begin to bake before he has got in the last. The little, age-old, iron lamp, sputtering and fluttering silently in its corner, shows him what he is about.

When the last loaf is properly placed, and the lamp withdrawn, the door is closed and the clock is set for the baking – fifty-five minutes should be right. The loaves come out the colour of ripe wheat or demerara sugar. The baker's daughter passes them through the open window swiftly to the baker, who, now clad in a grey homespun coat and demure grey hat, catches them and scrapes them to remove any traces of ashes from the oven. As he sets them down they crackle and 'snick' as they contract in the colder air.

The baker's boy has drawn up in the yard with the pony-and-trap, ready to take the load away, and children with coppers have come whistling down the cobbled path to fetch their mothers' special loaves. The baker's wife, a little lady with silver hair and silver-rimmed spectacles, comes in to slip a joint for the evening into the oven, 'so as not to waste the heat'.

Winter 1943

Not Eligible   Louise Ellis, Devon

A country baker had a reputation for excellent dough cakes, and a lady among his customers, hearing of this, ordered one. 'Why, ma'am,' said the scandalised baker, 'dough cakes aren't for the likes o' you. I only sells 'em to folks as eats wi' their elbows on the table'.

Winter 1965

An Ounce and a Half of Laudanum   by Ted Mills

It must be many years since a chemist in this country sold six-pennyworth of four-ha'porths, or threepennyworth of Parma violets, or an ounce and a half of laudanum – the odd half-ounce to tide the customer over a bank holiday. Yet in my apprentice days, just before 1914, such transactions would have been in no way remarkable. The laudanum was not in everyday demand; but there was no restriction on its sale, and no questions were asked. We had several 'regulars', opium addicts all, though we did not regard them as such or bother our heads as to how they got that way. As far as I know, neither did anybody else. It was not unknown for a fractious infant to get a drop or two of the stuff in his feeding-bottle. The 'four-ha'porths' was the universal family cough remedy – laudanum, paregoric, aniseed and peppermint in quantities carefully worked out by the chemist. Mixed with a pint of hot water and sugar, or black treacle, it dosed the family all winter and cheaply too, as it had to do in those days.

Life was rough, and we came up against it in many ways. I remember a dirty-looking old tramp asking in a cultured voice for threepennyworth of blue unction – strong ointment of mercury. He explained that circumstances were forcing him to sleep in common lodging-houses, where the fleas kept him awake all night. They came up from the bottom of the bed, he said, and this ointment smeared round the ankles kept them at bay. I am glad to remember that I did not charge him for it. Years later, in the army, I was obliged to use it myself and proved that it worked.

Though most of our customers were country folk, living a hard active life on the land, they were a constipated lot. We must have got rid of hundredweights of Epsom salts in a year, probably a ton or two if you included the cattle quality. There were people who made no distinction between medicines for cattle and those for humans, except to take the former in smaller doses. This was in the days before everything came ready packed, bottled, cartoned or cellophaned. The downtrodden middle-aged assistant and I did most of the packing between us on the premises. Each had a long list of drugs to be kept in half-pounds, quarters, two ounces or often, as with jalap, aloes and hiera picra (usually called 'hirapike'), in penny and twopenny packets. These three were purgatives.

We had to learn to be diplomatic. There was a substance called diachylon, looking like yellow rock. Melted in hot water it could be spread on cloth to make sticking plaster; roll plaster was then unknown. The same substance made into pills was used as a last hope in unwanted pregnancy; it was a toss-up which came first, lead poisoning or abortion. We always had to ask, 'What is it for?'

'A grubby pencilled note' (*George Adamson*)

When the glib answer came, 'To make plaster', we sold it, because it might have been true.

We kept a large number of perfumes, mostly floral and some good and wholesome, for sale at one-and-six an ounce, also eau-de-Cologne and lavender water at a shilling the ounce. Often early on a Saturday night some urchin would hand over a grubby pencilled note: '2d box Grossmith face powder, 2d Parma violets (in this bottle) and 1d carmine'. Somebody would say with a grin, 'Mum's going out tonight to earn the week's rent'.

Wednesday was market-day, and we knew it. It seemed as though all the countryside within a ten-mile radius flocked into town and stood three deep along the counter of our shop from ten till about four-thirty. A typical order would be for Epsom or Glauber's salts, bicarbonate of soda, cream of tartar, tartaric acid, linseed oil, turpentine, pickle spice, turmeric, vinegar and methylated spirit – all for one customer. We were lucky if we could grab a sandwich and ten minutes off.

We also made physic balls for horses and condition powders, udder ointment and mixed drenches for cows, and mange ointment for the farm dog. Making horse-balls was quite hard work, pounding the ingredients in a large iron mortar with stone pestle and hand-moulding them into small fat sausages. But we felt that we were only slightly remote from the soil, the farmers and their wives were good people to know and talk to, and in lots of small ways we had the satisfaction of helping things along. For seed-time we weighed up hundredweights of copper sulphate, all in one-pound bags for the farmers' convenience, even if the order was for fifty-six pounds.

The work was varied and interesting, but arduous. The long hours got me down; eight-thirty to eight on weekdays, 10 p.m. on Saturdays, one o'clock on Thursdays, if you had finished getting up the weekly order. Sometimes customers delayed us, and we lost a precious hour or more. I was a country boy and loved the open air, swimming, fishing, boating. In October 1914 I enlisted, and for the next four and a half years had all the fresh air I wanted. I was lucky and survived, but I never went back to shop life.

Spring 1971

As the Chemist Sees It   **Anonymous**

The village chemist enjoys the confidence of all kinds of people and is expected to have an encyclopaedic knowledge of every subject from cricket to theology. He is trusted implicitly to give the right medicines and receives many expressions of gratitude when they do good. As babies arrive, he must keep a watchful eye on their weights and be prepared to advise on feeding. Later, he must follow their progress through weaning to school-days, and always be ready to help with the usual childish ailments.

That at least has been my experience in the five years since I bought the chemist's shop in a village which, though largely residential, is several miles from a market-town. Among my neighbours are farmers, farm and forestry workers, poultry-keepers and smallholders, including a surprising number of educated ladies who manage, by perseverance and hard work seven days a week, to get a living from a few acres. But there are also retired people – military men, clergymen, civil servants, teachers and others. The village, which is mentioned in Domesday and even shows evidence of Roman settlement, now has a somewhat suburban appearance, but from my shop door I can watch men at work in the fields at all seasons of the year.

We live on the premises in a well-built modern house with an orchard-garden. The hours of business are long, for we provide what amounts to a day and night service, though in the winter months, when darkness falls (we have no street lamps) we might as well close the shop, but for the callers for medicines after evening surgery. When I am roused from my bed, or disturbed in my bath, to dispense an 'urgent' prescription, and am inclined to grumble, I recall the words of the Dorset countryman who, after losing his wife, exclaimed: 'Tain't no use bidin' an' mourning'; 'e dawn dew any good!'

One lady went to great pains to procure the correct bottle-teat: it had to be just the right length, shape and texture. In the end she bought a dozen and described how she fed a litter of pigs from twelve bottles fitted into a wooden holder, six on each side. The sale of veterinary medicines forms a fair proportion of our business: treatment for mastitis, cleansing drenches for cows, tonics for cattle in general, worming oils for pigs and coccidiosis treatment for poultry.

During my first summer in the village there were thousands of wasps, and practically every day I was besieged by customers asking for cyanide of potassium to destroy the nests. They requested it quite nonchalantly, as if they were asking for a box of patent pills. How was I, being new to the village, to conform to the poisons regulations, whereby the purchaser of such deadly stuff has to be known to the seller before he is allowed even to look at the poisons register? The same summer was a record one for ants, and I received much enlightenment from customers on their different antidotes: paraffin, borax, boiling water and the like.

There is a forthrightness and sense of humour in the village as a whole. On the one hand there are good-natured criticisms of the true villagers by the retired folk, and on the other sly digs by the villagers at neighbours, some of whom find it difficult to forget what they were before retirement and to live the life of normal country citizens. There is, too, much generosity and kindliness, so that no-one need feel lonely. Quite a number of old people live by themselves in their own cottages, valuing their independence, and if they are bedridden or helpless with rheumatism, a friendly neighbour will oblige with their shopping. Members of our Women's Institute looked after one old couple, both bedridden, and, on the death of the wife, assumed responsibility for the sale of the cottage and furniture and found a nursing-home for the husband.

The National Health Service is proving a great boon, particularly to these old people; some would not be alive today, were it not for the help of expensive drugs. 'You and I are helping to keep the old people alive' was the village doctor's comment to me the other day. He is sadly overworked, because the average age of the population is high and he has to cover a large and sparsely inhabited district.

The village grave-digger is a character. Outside the shop he was overheard to remark to a friend, as he watched a little man passing with whom he could not get on: ' 'E bain't lookin' so grand. I'm bidin' me time, got just the little corner for 'e'. One rugged Dorset farmer came in to buy some soap: 'None o' they fine scented soaps for me. They'm all right for the toffs, an' I sometimes gives the pigs a wash down with 'un, before a show; but I likes carbolic meself'. Another farmer whom I was able to help at one time picked me up in his car on my way back from the post office and handed me a chicken saying: 'Take this for the wife. I like you. You've got a nice face'.

Summer 1953

Mr Case the Draper   by Anthony Pearman

On Easter Sunday 1898, just after morning service, the bar parlour of the Royal Oak was comfortably filled by male members of the congregation. But why should General Booth be there? And why not in uniform but dressed in the box-hat and morning-coat of the ordinary church-going citizen? Yet there could not be any doubt that the broad high forehead, the prominent but well-shaped nose, piercing eyes and long white beard were those of the 'Army' chief. Moreover, he was finely criticising the music of the service just ended, telling the tenors just where they got off on the wrong foot in the anthem, and awarding praise and blame in the manner of an authority.

To the stranger looking on, the mystery remained unsolved until the following June, when a business call on Case the Draper, of Milborne St Andrew, revealed in the proprietor himself the General's double. Of upright stance and with confident manner, he presided over one of the strangest establishments to be found in rural Dorset.

Alone, in a shop with big sweeps of mahogany counter and fixtures to match, cedar-lined drawers gliding in or out at a touch with the smoothness of a century's use, Charles Case lived in the past. An examination of his stock would have revealed a number of the beaver box-hats beloved of John Leech, bales of shepherd's plaid, the fashionable cloth of the 1850s, and heavy materials, drapery and millinery of the same period, with a thin veneer of haberdashery, gloves and handkerchiefs spread over the museum pieces in an endeavour to appear up to date. Not that he was a mere village shopkeeper, for he and his brothers had learned their trade long ago in the London warehouses, 'spending money like water', as the older inhabitants remarked. Certainly there were few who had more vivid memories of the theatres of the period, when the boys were picking up their trade and a knowledge of city night-life. And now, in his hale old age and unique surroundings, he was a relic not only of a once prosperous business but also of a defunct home industry.

Until the mid-1850s the linen and cotton buttons in use throughout the land were made mainly in the cottage-homes of Dorset, and Charles Case's father was agent and buyer for the London trade of a large proportion of their output. With farm-worker's wages at 9s per week, mother, an expert buttoner, often doubled the family income, and the rush to obtain work was so great that, on the fortnightly handing-in day, the village was like a fair; women crowded in from farm and cottage anywhere within a six-mile radius. So extensive was the demand that a relative of the Cases made a good living by merely drawing the wires which formed the foundations of the buttons; they used a rustless alloy, the secret of which has long been lost.

When I knew Charles Case, he still treasured a remnant of the tokens issued by his father. Workers who had travelled a certain distance could obtain bread and cheese to the value of 2d and a pint of beer at the 'Oak' or one of the other village hostelries. Mr Case strongly denied that truck had any part in those transactions, but added naïvely, 'Of course, in giving out the work, we naturally favoured those who were good customers in the shop'.

The transport of the finished goods was a business in itself. The father found the coach service and goods wagons not always reliable and had a special vehicle built for the purpose, a light wagonette with the driver's seat in front and a body honeycombed with sliding drawers, each of which held a gross of cards of buttons, classified according to shapes and sizes so that they cound be handed out expeditiously. The old gentleman would drive this to London once a month, taking just a week for the double journey, with a couple of days going round the warehouses.

It was on one such expedition that he found yet another way of increasing his profits. He was offered by chance a job lot of clothing which had just gone out of fashion in town and, rightly thinking that rural Dorset would be at least one season behind the city in its styles, he not only bought the lot but bargained for its repetition each year. This answered well until his customers woke up to the fact that they were behind the times. When at last this happened he was equal to the occasion, for he bought the out-of-date stuff in greater quantities than ever and shipped it from Poole to the Newfoundland Fisheries, where the sparse inhabitants clamoured for it as the latest from London.

He prospered thus, until it seemed that he had the Midas touch and all his transactions ended in double profits. But the end came suddenly. On his return from one of his usual trips to town, at the beginning of the 1860s, he slammed down on the counter, with the words, 'That's the end of the Dorset button trade', a card of the new machine-made buttons from a factory in the north of England. These could be sold at a quarter of the cost price of the ones made locally by hand.

With the abrupt end of their industry, the poor of the heart of Dorset experienced real distress. The Cases, too, were sorely hit, but there was still hope for them because a large part of their spare capital was invested in the Poole trade, in which the 'Fire-fly' bore to Newfoundland a larger stock of drapery than ever before. Hopes were raised as the time of her arrival drew nearer, to be gradually diminished as she became overdue and month succeeded month with no news of her. Finally she was adjudged a total loss, and the cargo was not insured. Then the local bank, where the remnant of the Cases' capital was deposited, suspended payment and avoided bankruptcy only by the narrowest margin. The old gentleman never recovered from these repeated blows of fortune and died within a few weeks of the last of them.

Since that time Charles Case had largely lived not only in but on the past. For some unknown reason quantities of old envelopes had been stored away, and now their black penny stamps acquired a collector's value; a few of the Mulready envelopes that preceded postage stamps proper added to the worth of the find. As years went by, Dorset buttons became museum pieces so that there was a slight revival in their sale. The tokens, too, fetched more than their original value, and the pair of flint-lock pistols carried to London for fear of highwaymen at last found a use that they never had previously. Above all, pieces of furniture, well bought in the family's period of prosperity – Chippendale, Sheraton and other noted makes – would occasionally fetch fancy prices at local auctions. So Mr Case lived to a placid old age, happy in his recollection of past grandeur and in his neighbours' respect.

Shortly before his death, he came out, with most of the villagers, to welcome the real General Booth, then on a motor-tour in the West Country. As they gazed on one another, it was as if each twin had found his long-lost brother.

Spring 1952

Market Bookstore   by Alan Walbank

The square was full of farmers with pigs and calves in straw-bedded trailers, crowded among stalls of fruit, harness, hardware and fish. The market-hall was a bazaar of oriental carpets, cloth remnants, rolls of silk flourished by hucksters to the farmers' wives. Trussed fowls, duck eggs, farm cheeses competed in plump appeal with rounds of yellow butter impressed with a cow's head. The usual kind of market-day in any one of half a dozen small towns of the Yorkshire dales.

In one retired corner of the square there was a different stall or rather one-room shop, squeezed under a solicitor's office between the grocer's and the tailor's. Its door stood wide; its walls and window space were stacked with books. There was no-one in attendance, no bell. A plate with some silver and copper lay on the carved oak table. On the shelves was a mixture of all sorts, from heavy volumes on lead mining and three-decker Victorian novels to pamphlets on cheese-making and gatherings of light verse. As I browsed, another customer came in, nearer to seventy than sixty and handier, from his appearance, with a drover's stick or a billhook than with a book. Delving in a back shelf near the floor, he fetched up a dusty tome and remarked at large: 'Ah thowt ah'd find it here: it'll save a mort of argufying o' Sunday', then placed a coin on the plate and thrust back among the pigs and calves. From the company it had kept his find seemed to be a theological work, and I could see him triumphantly clinching his point with the local preacher.

This book-store, open on market-day and Saturday or, if you are in the know, by obtaining a key from either the grocer or the tailor, is probably unique. The owner's hobby is book-collecting, and partly to relieve his overflowing shelves, partly to secure a retreat from business for a chat with other book-lovers, he unloads here the unwanted items of sales bundles. The system it to take your choice and pay what you think right: local people use it as a sort of unofficial lending library. What is one likely to find? My search unearthed Thackeray in orginal cloth, Fielding, a two-volume Gothic novel in marbled boards and morocco labels, Defoe, Bunyan, a row of Victorian 'yellowbacks' and what a habitué called 'the finest selection of poetry in this part of the world'. A sprinkling of more modern novels, art series and guide books garnished the window. One browser, on a visit from Australia, found a long-sought childhood favourite and its sequel, and gladly offered a pound for the pair. The reply was: 'Dost tha think ah'm going to have you come here from Australia to be robbed?' and the acceptance of a shilling.

Winter 1962

The Ironmonger's Hoard   by Katharine Pindar

A stock of ironmongery dating from the nineteenth century was found scattered through shop premises in Presteigne in Wales early last year. There were scores of tin kettles and teapots, some Victorian cast-iron mantelpieces, bicycle bells, brass knobs, and boot buttons, to mention only a few of the goods found.

The owner of the shop, 98-year-old Mr Newell, was still making a profit in the 200-year old family business selling modern ironmongery, when he died in January 1973. The huge hoard of old goods, mostly kept in unopened brown paper packets, was found when auctioneers came in to deal with the property.

Then many of the dusty packets of nails and hairpins, bottles and tins, might have been consigned to the local rubbish dump, had not a Burford antique dealer, Roger Warner, patiently collected them up. The premises were large and the old stock scattered through twelve store rooms. An assortment of candle-snuffers was found quite near an entrance; but it was only during his final check that Mr Warner uncovered a collection of tin cones with handles which were used for mulling ale.

The shop was founded in 1770, but the bulk of the old stock dated from ninety to a hundred years later. It had been super-seded and forgotten. The business had included some manufacturing, among other goods, of tin-ware, but tin was mainly replaced by enamel. Wire blinds, clocks and watches were also made.

The old stock included among many other curious items, a brass roasting jack, a wooden carpenter's brace, a fire extinguisher consisting of a glass tube full of water, a monster pair of horse hair clippers, a small suspended weighing machine, a travelling metal boot jack, wrought iron baskets to carry fire ashes, lead bullets and rare horse-hair fishing floats, a cork compressor and boxes of corks, and a humane mouse trap that caught the mouse without killing it. A touch of colour was provided by old-fashioned enamelled advertisements, for sporting tackle and furniture polish and razors, bicycles and lawn mowers and incandescent gas mantles.

Roger Warner took all the old stock away and laid it out in the cellar of his Burford shop. 'This is the sort of thing sensible antique dealers don't do but I always do,' he confessed. It had taken a great deal of time to sort out the goods. Time was always the problem, in going through old hoards in private homes as well as shops; it can still happen that old relics are consigned to rubbish dumps.

But Mr Newell's ironmongery is not only saved, it is to be kept together. The old man had determined that the family business should be continued for 200 years, although he had no family to succeed him, and he achieved his aim. Now his stock will remain intact in the Folk Museum of Wales at St Fagan's Castle, near Cardiff. Mr Warner might have sold it much more profitably, but he said 'It's gone where I want it.'

So the public will be able to see the ironmongery that lay unopened for a century, displayed as it might have been in the Newells' shop in 1870. And perhaps the publicity may lead to a few more old stocks of goods being saved for the nation instead of being dispersed or dumped.

Spring 1974

General Dealer   by Ewan Clarkson

Ikey's yard, some people say, is a disgrace; and the council should do something about it. Yet if it were not for Ikey and his brethren in the trade, the countryside would become increasingly untidy, for he makes a living out of the stuff other people throw away – rusty iron, old bedsteads, bicycle frames, rags, sacks, wooden boxes, bottles, barbed wire and derelict vehicles of all kinds. It is not a comfortable living, still less a lucrative one. Jan, the market gardener, sold Ikey the boiler that had been broken by the frost, and he was pleased to get a fiver for it. When he heard that Ikey had sold it for £10 he was convinced he had been exploited; but he did not have to smash the cast iron into little pieces, load it on a lorry and drive it fifteen miles to Exeter. I helped Ikey on that occasion; he gave me £2 of his profit, and never did I work so hard for forty shillings.

Ikey's terms are strictly cash. On buying – a process which may be prolonged and complicated – he will, when a price is finally agreed, pace nervously to and fro for a few moments, as though panic-stricken at his own temerity. Then, from the bib pocket of his greasy overalls, he will produce a fat roll of notes, peel off the right number and hand them over, often with the promise that if he does well out of the deal there will be a few more shillings to come. The cynical have been pleasantly surprised when, weeks or months later, the promise has been fulfilled.

When selling, Ikey is even more eccentric. Pressed for the price of an article, he will at first deny all knowledge of its worth. Then he will tell you with disarming honesty what he paid for it, adding 'Give me a drink on top of that'. A 'drink' would appear to be roughly ten per cent of the purchase price. He will smash an article with his biggest sledge-hammer rather than give it away to someone who, he knows, can well afford to pay; but he will give up hours of his time to anyone who is struggling, grumbling the while at his own stupidity.

His daily transactions are an income-tax collector's nightmare. I have known him accidentally kill a chicken in his yard, swop it for 12lb of tomatoes, then, nearer the coast, trade half the tomatoes for a string of mackerel and, on the way home, exchange some of these for a pound of butter. One summer day I helped him take a rotovator from one farm to another, where we picked up a shed. This we delivered to a third farm, where we collected a concrete mixer. It went to a builder's yard, where a quantity of timber and some bags of cement were waiting for us to load. These were then delivered to the farm where we had collected the rotovator. The financial adjustments involved in that day's work made my head reel.

Though never without transport in his life, Ikey has not owned a new vehicle. Indeed, only when a machine has come to resemble a battered cocoa tin has he any faith in its reliability. He is a shortish man and his dress, through constant contact with rust and grease, leaves much to be desired. His only status symbols are the roll of notes in his breast pocket – his working capital – and, when he calls on a wealthy stranger to negotiate a biggish deal, his cigar. On these occasions he will send his mate ahead with the lorry to announce his imminent arrival, so that his grand entrance, cigar at full blast like a miniature furnace, may create the maximum impression.

A reputable man, working extremely hard in what some might consider a disreputable trade: a staunchly independent little man. Without him we would all be a good deal untidier, and some of us poorer.

Spring 1965

Country Garage   by Arnold Handley

My garage stands on the site of an old forge; and the comparison between a country garage and a blacksmith's shop is often drawn. Maybe it is true, but not in the way you think. Modern memories of the village blacksmith are coloured by nostalgia: he was a man among men, a gentle giant, wise and patient, strong and skilled. He was more than a blacksmith; he represented an age of uncomplicated morality, when every man knew his place. We usurpers are representatives of giant international oil cartels with a brand image of ultra-modern commercialism. Times change; but men don't. The blacksmith and I work for the same object – money. Our long working hours are devoted to earning it, our sleepless nights to thinking of ways to get it.

A country garage's basic problem arises from the low population density. Petrol sales on a major road running through the countryside may be smaller than those on a suburban road; and even when they are greater, a country garage relying on petrol sales alone would be running at a slight loss. It is sales of tyres, batteries, accessories and oil that pay the wages. The profit on a motor-cycle battery is about the same as that on thirty gallons of petrol: thirty times out in the cold, switch on, felt pad over the tank, wait while he fumbles through layers of clothing for the money, get the change, probably check the tyres. Selling petrol is a slow way of getting rich. The greater population density in towns allows a higher proportion of accessory to petrol sales;

there are more pedestrians to see the window displays – more impulse buys. And the unsociability of townsfolk pushes up profit per hours worked. It is, 'A quid's worth, mate' and, if he is feeling talkative, 'Ta', then away.

The charm of a country garage lies in its customers, who are individuals and not just drivers mouthing petrol orders from behind closed car windows. My charm wears thin towards the end of the day, for we work from 7.30 in the morning to between 10 and 11 at night: that is, fourteen or fifteen hours a day, seven days a week, because the profit margin is not large enough to allow for adequate staff. After about 9 in the evening I begin to drop spanners and give wrong change. I lose track of what day it is; the predominant feeling is tiredness. The pump lights go out at 10.30, and I am in bed by 10.33: no chit-chat, no late night shows, no drinking till the pubs close – bed.

The bane of a small business is bad debts and, if anything can keep me awake, they can. Countless small firms have gone down under the burden of customers who would not pay their bills. People who would never dare to carry anything away from a chain store in town without paying take for granted that they can have goods on credit in the country. It is not dishonesty; it is thoughtlessness. I wonder what the village blacksmith heard as the equivalent of 'Do you know, I don't seem to have my cheque-book on me'.

A town garage meets downright dishonesty, forged cheques, deliberate swindlers; but in the stockbroker belt the trouble is slow payment. I am not as badly hit as some of my competitors, for I run no petrol credit accounts. They hinder a business. In theory all is fine but, human nature being what it is, a man would rather pay me £1 every other day than receive a bill for £35 at the end of the month. He argues that £1 every other day does not come to £35 in a month. It does not cheer him to learn that the bill includes a tyre and his wife's cigarettes, and that his son has learned the magic password, 'Charge it to our account'. His resentment washes off on to the garage, and a customer and bill are lost. How I envy the garage with a notice in the workshop, 'No car is to be taken away unless paid for'! How could I say that to my neighbours? The result is that a man with a guilty conscience over a £2 repair bill buys his petrol elsewhere for a while until he can pay me. Again credit loses profit.

This is a tough competitive business; there is no more rural lethargy about it than about broiler chickens or market gardening. On most 'A' roads there are about ten garages every nine miles, each struggling to get the custom of one per cent of the traffic passing on that side of the road, because few drivers will cross over for petrol. A big sales drive might increase business to two per cent; it is a good garage that gets more.

Strangely enough, it is this difficulty of gaining business that I enjoy. Life in a suburban semi-detached would be dull after a job where my weekly pay is directly proportionate to my sales-manship. A long time ago, when I did live in a semi-detached, tending my little garden on a Saturday, I would straighten up and see all my neighbours tending their little gardens and picture myself striding with gun-dogs at my heels across my own acres. Now that I have got five or six acres I doubt if I ever step off the garage forecourt.

The mammoth oil company, which paints my pumps and gives free overalls in return for my not selling competitors' oils, lives in a London skyscraper. It would fit into my forecourt with room to spare. Is there a moral there? If so, I cannot just think what it is.

Winter 1963

No Room at the Pub   by William Clarke

Recently I revisited Gloucestershire, to hunt up my grandfather with whom I had lost contact for a number of years. I arrived in the village around lunch-time and decided to look in first at the pub opposite the station. It was there, I recalled, that I was most likely to find him at that time of day.

I was immediately struck by the number of cars parked in the forecourt, where I had been used to see an old banger or two and the occasional truck from some neighbouring farm or market-garden. I thought that some kind of business conference might be taking place inside, and this seemed to be confirmed when I entered what was once the saloon and had now been redesignated 'The Snuggery': the place was crowded with sleek young executives and their sleeker secretaries. They were all chatting ninety to the dozen, forking hors-d'oeuvres from plastic plates and absent-mindedly sipping lager, white wine, and a quite amazing variety of spirits.

The interior had been altered out of all recognition. The old oak panelling had been replaced by the silkiest and most expensive vinyl wall-paper. The once-plain deal floor-boards were everywhere lushly carpeted, and the bar itself might well have been transferred straight from the Folies-Bergère. Nor was there anyone there I recognised, either one side of the counter or the other.

I corkscrewed my way to where the beer-handles used to be, and after much painful gesturing managed to attract the attention of what looked like the local bank manager deputizing for the landlord. There were two or three pretty young receptionists there too, obviously enjoying themselves playing at being barmaids as a change from the usual dull office routine.

I ordered half a pint of keg bitter (there seemed to be no other kind available), and had it drawn up for me by the bank manager as grudgingly as if my request had been for an overdraft. 'You wouldn't happen to know if old Tom Roberts is around anywhere, would you?' I asked in the tone of one completely inhibited by his surroundings.

The landlord (let us settle for that) regarded me as disdainfully as if I had just been mucking out the pigs. 'We get very few old people in here now,' he observed, with a decided sniff. 'Would it happen to be one of the local inhabitants you were looking for?'

I was trying to locate my grandfather, I said. He had lived for the better part of seventy years in one of those old cottages down by the millpond, and to the best of my knowledge was living there now. The landlord was sorry he could not help me. That he was not a bit sorry was obvious, and I got the impression that he was blissfully unaware of the existence of either cottages or millponds.

It was no use appealing to anyone else. They were all strangers to the neighbourhood, as far as I could tell. Maybe my grandfather had been consigned to the public bar round the back, through the alley by the Gents. There was no public bar, how-

Then and Now   by **Brian Walker**

The ploughman's lunch . . .

Spring 1977

ever, no alley, and (as far as I could see) no Gents. One thing I did notice, though, was a framed menu card by the door indicating that I could obtain a most exotic luncheon in 'The Olde Tappe Room' for £2.50 (plus VAT). I decided I was not all that hungry.

Two of the five cottages were still where they used to be and one of them was my grandfather's, though the millpond was now a car park. I knocked repeatedly, then pulled on the bootlace that had given unwarranted entry from time immemorial. But there was no one at home.

Old Jack Rumble was still around though. He was coming out of one door as I closed the other, and apologised for not recognising me on account of his eyes getting worse every week. I would find old Tom in the churchyard, he said; and when even he could not fail to observe my reaction he assured me that grandfather was only visiting. 'Goes up there to get away from the blasted traffic,' he said. 'It's been something dreadful since they opened up the new road.'

That was where I found him, after taking ten minutes to cross what I once skipped over in seconds. He was squatting on the marble doorstep of one of our late worthies, clutching one of those ring-cans of beer with another on the grass at his feet.

'Hallo, son,' he exclaimed. 'Just having a quiet drink and a chat with a few old friends. Don't know anywhere else I can do that now.'

I should have been shocked, I suppose, considering it was to that church, through that churchyard, I used to be dragged regularly to Matins and Evensong, to say nothing of Sunday School in between. In actual fact I could not help chuckling to myself over those cans of beer. 'Bet he didn't get them from the Snuggery or the Olde Tappe Room,' I thought. 'More likely from the local Supermarket.'

Autumn 1976

At Your Service

Wooing the Thatcher by Joyce Ward

He gazed at me unblinking, his blue eyes washed pale by all weathers as a sailor's are by the sea.

'Oh, ah,' he said with grave deliberation, and became absorbed in rolling a bent cigarette with gnarled fingers.

'So you might manage that?' I queried as I shivered in the biting East Anglian wind of a bitter February day. The thick clay of his garden dragged clammily at my frozen feet, but stand fast I must and would.

'Just a *small* cottage. One dormer at the back and two at the front. I don't imagine it would take long to do? Of course, I realise that the weather is the first consideration – but as it happens I can wait until May and it is often beautiful then.'

He nodded almost imperceptibly.

'Perhaps I could help with transport?' I suggested. 'Seven miles is no joke.'

He looked so slight, almost frail, with his white hair blowing from under his cap and his heavily booted feet appearing two sizes too big for his spindly legs. And the push-bike leaning up against the shed was evidently his only vehicle.

Thoughtfully he cleared his throat as a preliminary to speech.

'Which May?' he asked.

'Why, this one!' I cried. 'Two months from now – or say almost three.'

The thatcher pulled thoughtfully at the lobe of one of his bright red ears.

'I'll ha' to see,' he conceded in a tone of finality that clearly ended the interview.

In the first week of May I heard from Mr Trim – for incredibly enough that was his name, in Happy Family fashion – to this effect: 'I got work to July when I will fit in your work if poss. A. Trim. Thatcher.' It was some consolation that the builders working on the cottage were behindhand too. One of them, an under-sized Cockney immigrant, buzzed busily about like a bee from another hive; but his hefty rural mates took things slowly, as turnips grow in the wide fields at predestined pace.

By the beginning of July the new dormers had taken shape, staring wide-eyed through the old shabby thatch. The time had come. I set forth, and found the thatcher digging in his garden. He straightened up slowly, pushed his cap to the back of his silver head and announced:

'Can't get no straw.'

'No straw! What can you mean?' I was aghast.

'Farmer I goo to, he's give up long straw. I dunno where to turn and that's the trewth. Mayhap yew know o' long straw your way? That I don't and that's a fact.'

'Me? No, certainly not,' I protested – yet felt flattered at this childlike confidence in my varied capacities. 'But leave it with me, Mr Trim. I shall be in touch,' I added. He reached a leisurely hand for his spade and turned back to his garden plot.

A fortnight of intensive staff work followed, with heavily-subsidised spies in the shape of roadmen, postmen, barmen and the local poacher. Then success! Twelve miles from the cottage a farmer had a field of long straw, ripe for action and only half of it needed for his barns.

Triumphant, exulting, I bore down upon Mr Trim with the happy news.

'I've got the straw, Mr Trim! Delivery next week!' I shouted from the gate. He turned reflectively from the roses he was dousing with soapy washing-up water.

'Oh ah?' he said and bent to finish his task.

Five days later, looking up from my own rose-bed, I beheld something like a haystack preceded by huffs and puffs of blue smoke lumbering towards me down the lane. The straw! It lurched hugely to a standstill at the gate and a cheerful voice called: 'Oi! here it are!' The tractor driver beamed at me through smoke, sweat and straw, and from the stack itself slid two nut-brown gypsies who began at once to build a straw-stack in my front garden.

I collected Mr Trim, his bike and his tools the next day. We

'A haystack preceded by huffs and puffs . . .' (*Brian Walker*)

drove awhile in silence. Then he cleared his throat preparatory to speech.

'Can't do little but sort the straw,' he stated. 'Got no sticks.'

'No sticks?'

'Fer splittin'. Got ta hev sticks else yer can't start. Hazel, fit for soakin'. I gotta place I goo up the woods.'

'Well, I say, do go and get them!' I pressed him anxiously. 'Why not?'

'Along o' the pheasants. Can't get up the wood,' he answered lugubriously, and began slowly to roll one of his strangely shaped cigarettes.

A fortnight crawled by before he responded to my urging to rove farther afield for his sticks. Followed another fortnight when he sat interminably in my garage deftly whittling them, and September came.

Then the thatcher asked for an afternoon from my time to repair with a patch a 'widder-woman's' roof. With good grace I drove him to a tiny cottage beside the village green and after tea went to collect him back.

'Ah,' the old lady informed me, 'he's been took home. Me

The thatching in progress (*Brian Walker*)

ladder give way and 'is arm's hurt. Finished me roof first, thank
the Lord.'

He came back in October. I had become a harder character,
largely through his training. I arranged to fetch him next morning – to ensure his early arrival – and did so. 'We will take your
bike in the back, Mr Trim,' I told him in a tone not brooking
argument, 'so you can return under your own steam.' He looked
satisfied rather than otherwise. Suffice to say that every midday
that bike took wings and carried Mr Trim from my cottage to the
Five Bells up the hill. Unhurriedly he freewheeled back.

But at last the glorious day came when Mr Trim climbed his
long ladder, dug his leather-capped knees into the roof and
positively set about it.

At once he was transformed. Gone the frail, bent, evasive old
man one met at ground level. Here instead was a spry, intent
craftsman, content and at one with his straw and the wide skies
and the weather, absorbed in his work and with beautiful economy
of effort. When I bellowed: 'Teatime, Mr Trim!' he would not
hear for a while, then give a jaunty wave. Down his ladder he
came to his mug of tea and wedge of sandwich. The carpenter

and plasterer would conduct their friendly arguments, while the thatcher – earth-bound once more – munched morosely and silently, his pale eyes fixed on the ground at his feet or raised to rove over the roof, studying it straw by straw.

Once I asked the Cockney sprite how they hit it off together. 'Me and Fred fine and dandy. Trim he's a lone-rider.'

It rained, it blew and in December it froze, and the straw was too wet, too 'playful' or too brittle. In the intervals the roof grew – slowly, how slowly! – and the straw-stack diminished. In like proportion, Mr Trim seemed larger up there on the roof, being encased in three waistcoats – one ex-Sunday-suit, one railway porter's cast-off of thick blue-serge, and one army-surplus leather.

Flashes of encouragement came now and then. 'Startin' her eyebrows termorrer.' Oh wizardry of embroidered thatch above the dormers!

'Be on the ridge Monday.' And astride he sat, knees gripping, deft hands sculpting straw.

On the twenty-eighth of February, with family, friends and villagers, I stood back to see and to admire the finished effect. Our praises rang upon the frosty air.

The thatcher seemed unmoved or deaf to the compliments abounding. For a fleeting second one might have caught a deep satisfaction in the pale eyes as they contemplated the lovely roof, trim as his name and appealing as new-baked bread.

He carefully gathered up the remaining straw and distributed it over the recumbent bicycle in the back of my car – which will be straw-strewn for ever.

Where the stack had stood so long in the garden the grass was sickly-pale and flattened. But everywhere tiny yellow shoots were pushing bravely up.

'Soon goo rarely green,' he observed, 'Yew'll hev a tidy lot of daffs where that straw's bin a-covering 'em and warmin' 'em threw.'

Mr Trim was the gardener once more, mindful of spring in whatever year it happened to be.

Winter 1976

A Thatcher on Thatch   by Jeremy Burnett

As I were out in mead last week,
A-thatchen o' my little rick,
There green young ee-grass, ankle-high,
Did sheen below the cloudless sky;
An' over hedge in togher groun',
Among the bennets dry an' brown,
My dun wold meare, wi' neck a-freed
Vrom Zummer work, did snort an' veed;
An' in the sheade o' leafy boughs
My vew wold ragged-cwoated cows
Did rub their zides upon the rails,
Or switch 'em wi' their heairy tails.

A thatched house and rick, a green meadow, a hazel covert, a few cows, the occasional cackle of hens, mingled perhaps with the smell of pigs: all can be found anywhere in the countryside, from East Anglia to Cornwall, and be enjoyed, as William Barnes enjoyed them, by anyone interested enough to travel a few miles from his city home or office. More and more people are retiring to find the pleasanter aspects of country life; but I wonder how many will really become a part of it. Surely there is a great gulf between the person who weeds his garden, counts the different wild flowers down the lane and perhaps contributes regularly to the 'Country Corner' of his local paper, and the man who can lean on a field gate and decide whether or not a particular patch of land should be put down to grass; whether a tractor or a good old Suffolk Punch should pull the plough; and whether it would be advisable to thatch the cottage in Norfolk reed or long straw. Is this man not as much a part of the landscape as a chicken or a cow? It was a longing to be part of something which is full of interest, surprises, disappointments, poverty and riches (and perhaps a complete inability to learn anything academic) that first dragged me from the indecision of the middle teens to reed, spars and cider.

I now have a 12-cwt van. My father, when he started his own business in the early 'twenties, had a pony and cart; but like him, whenever I am out with my family on the road passing farms and cottages I have thatched, we talk of little else but whether such-and-such a roof is wearing well or not. Having thatched a roof, I

Some ancient trades have made a comeback – thatching in particular. Little has changed as these pictures of Mr Edwards, a thatcher of Bucknell, Shropshire, (*Ted Picken*) and Mr Lewis of West Winterside, Hampshire, (*George H. Hall*) show. Photographed in about 1900 and 1972 respectively, the main differences are in the clothes and the ladders.

regard it as my possession and feel responsible for its well-being. I have had some heated arguments with clients who have allowed creepers to run riot over not only the walls of their cottages but also the roofs. This has the same effect on thatch as if one were to clout a pile of tiles with a sledge-hammer. Another cause of friction is the habit of pushing television aerials through the thatch: it cannot be done with a tiled roof, so why do it with a thatched one?

Every thatcher I meet has this same personal approach to his work, perhaps because it is his life and not just another job. This, I think, is thatch's strongest weapon against the contractor, who is in business solely to make money. At the moment thatch is just managing to hold its own against its many enemies – not least local authorities, who encourage the owners of many old and beautiful cottages to rip off their thatch and cover the roofs with

asbestos tiles or some other synthetic horror, so that once picturesque dwellings look like rather unhygienic public conveniences.
I am sure that, if a small grant – say, ten per cent – were available
to property owners for complete rethatching, we would see the
thatcher not only holding his own among our older buildings, but
also making great inroads into modern housing estates; and even
his re-establishment as 'perhaps the most important of the hamlet
craftsmen', as Richard Jefferies once described him. I believe
that a grant of this nature would result in an increase of at least
fifteen per cent in the number of thatched dwellings in the next
ten years. This would enable us to bring on more apprentices and
lead eventually to a great reduction in charges, for out of every
£100 of our turnover £10 has to be spent on transport. As I
write, I have to work out an estimate for rethatching a house in
West Cornwall; and I live in Norfolk. There is a real danger that,
unless the use of thatch increases, the local hallmarks of the trade
will completely disappear, leaving one type of thatcher, working
(as now in some parts) as one of a gang of men.

Apart from the cost, the would-be owner of a thatched house
is deterred by the exceedingly high rates charged by nearly all
insurance companies – 15s per cent, compared with the usual 5s
or 6s. Yet what real additional risk is there? Surely when a fire
reaches the roof of a building, what is left is not worth saving.
And you cannot start a fire on a roof of thatch with a cigarette
or any amount of sparks; I have tried. Steam-engines were once
the greatest danger because, when stoking up, they had a habit of
ejecting red-hot cinders and, if these landed on thatch, it might
smoulder for hours before bursting into flame. But how many
steam-engines are there on the roads today?

Thatch is sometimes blamed for another type of fire, for which
it is in no way responsible. When an old house or cottage is
bought by a town dweller – or for that matter by a countryman
– usually the first thing that happens is the gutting and renewal
of the interior. The old open fireplace that will swallow a faggot
of wood, where a fire will burn night and day for years on end, is
replaced by a modern stove that needs attention only once a day,
has a forced draught and looks nice and tidy. In many of these
old buildings the roof timbers run right through the chimney.

This did not matter when the fireplace was open, but with the stove's forced draught a spark may be blown up on to a beam and fanned persistently; and the timber may smoulder for weeks before fire finally spreads to the rest of the building. To my personal knowledge this caused the complete destruction of three cottages; and on each occasion the thatch was blamed instead of the man who put the lump of ironmongery in a place where only stone, cob, timber and reeds had a right to be.

Perhaps the most irritating enemy of thatch, and the most difficult to fight, is the person who describes it as 'old-fashioned, dirty and full of fleas and rats'. Let me make it quite clear that thatch is no more old-fashioned than America's Atlas rocket; that it is no dirtier than the garden vegetables we eat, and that in my nine years' experience I have yet to find either a flea or a rat in it. On several occasions I have found traces of rats on the upper side of ceilings, but surely this reflects on those people who leave scraps of food around. There has been no evidence of rats having penetrated a roof, so I suppose they must have come up through the house.

Last summer we moved from our tiny two-up, two-down cottage on the fringe of Exmoor to the somewhat colder and drier climate of the Brecklands of Norfolk. Here we have a good farmhouse and five acres of land. We came not out of choice – my wife and I with our family could enjoy living in the country anywhere – but of necessity. During the first few years I have been doing an ever increasing number of jobs for people who have not the means to pay for their roofs. Now, if work is not paid for, we will at least be able to live off the smallholding. There is a wonderful barn which will be ideal for winter brotch making, and there appears to be no shortage of either material or work. Although a great deal of my time will still be spent in the West Country, our Breckland acres will be our stronghold for many years to come.

The future of thatch will long remain a question for debate, as my father tells me it was when he was a boy. One thing to my mind is certain; thatch must either make progress or disappear completely from the country scene. This would take two to three hundred years at least, for more than half the world's population still lives a full and comfortable life under what was probably the first form of roofing devised by man.

I have three boys at home. Philip, aged seven, comes in saying there's a thatched house on the way to school, but it isn't any good because they have had to put wire netting over it. Paul, aged five, wants to be a thatcher because then he would be a 'real workman'. Roger, aged eleven months, has not yet voiced his opinion. Nothing would please me more than to see them follow me 'up the ladder'; but they must choose for themselves, because if local authorities, insurance companies and the like are not brought to their senses pretty soon, earning one's living at the trade will become, to say the least, extremely dicey. I wonder if that is why my wife is trying to get me to earn our winter keep by becoming a journalist.

Summer 1962

Thatching with Father   by Jack Brown

The writer was born at the turn of the century in the village of Castle Camps on the Cambridgeshire-Essex border and moved with his family at an early age to Great Bardfield. He describes his father as 'a tall saturnine man with lean face, fresh complexion and close dark brows. His nose was of an orange-like 'texture', slightly enlarged at the end, and under his clean-shaven upper lip he carried a diagonal scar. His lips had a certain thickness and were often pursed, monkey-like. On his chin was a small boatman-type tuft of hair. His grey-green eyes were of the staring, penetrating kind and could appear somewhat luminous. Heavily booted, he wore the inevitable corduroys, which were usually tied at the knees, and a strong grey waistcoat with an old brass watch-chain looped to a pocket in the top of the cords, where his gun-metal watch reposed. Above the waistcoat a vee of Oxford shirting, patched but clean, showed round his bare throat. A heavy tweed coat completed his attire, apart from a dark bowler which rested squarely on his greying head, and the inevitable red handkerchief'. As a thatcher and tier of hay and straw, he was a master-man, unshackled by social ties, self-reliant, albeit uneducated. To his eldest son he appeared as a 'hard Victorian parent, storming his way through life, kicking against the pricks, cheated and frustrated at every turn of the hard way; battling against Nature's elements with a belly full of cold meat, pickles and a pint of beer'.

Father had designs on me long before I reached my teens, always grudging me the security of enforced hours at school. He would have my sister Annie out too, twisting straw bands and drawing out wet straw from the 'bed' for thatching. My small hand soon became quite tough through handling the various tools of his trade, the inside joints of my fingers showing pads of yellow corny flesh. I copied other boys and whittled away at these with a pocket-knife. My forearms also became sore with the constant brushing of straw as I quartered it into yelms.

Pulling double handfuls of wet straw from a heap, forming a neat straight row from right to left, may appear elementary, but there is much more to it than that. Your head is near the ground in the quartering part of the job. I was often assailed by sickness when, with lowered head, I got a smell of the wet straw, which made me retch. Right – left – left – right – pat – comb – thump went my hands, as I shuffled steadily forward. The yelms, gathered into tight armfuls, had to be pinched and squeezed in the picking up, and this is where a strong chest helped. They were packed firmly in a stout wooden holder – a dog we called it – with the ends crossed a little to keep each one separate for laying in the course on the roof. The resulting bundle was then tied tightly, under knee and muscle, by the cord attached to the dog. After trimming it at both ends by pulling out loose straws, I was ready for Father's shout from the roof, as an empty dog came hurtling down to be refilled. With a double swing I got the bulky bundle across my shoulder, high up, grasping the jutting ends of the dog. Hey, hup! and off I went, holding the ladder baulk tightly with my right hand and keeping a grip on the dog with my left.

When dizziness forced me to give in, Father always said I was bilious. 'Sit down a bit. Bin eatin' b——— sweets. Ya'll soon git over it.' Glad to rest in the dry straw for a spell, I would sense him hurrying into work in an effort to fill the gap I had caused. He was more anxious about that than over my personal sufferings, and before long he would ask after my health, more in anger than in sorrow. 'Don't ya feel better now?' he would command, while my little bit of world, with the nasty tangy bed of wet straw as a blurry centre-piece, whirled round before my half-closed eyes. 'Ye-es', I would answer uncertainly. 'Well, soon as ya can, git another bed ready. Ya won't have ya head down so much doin' that.'

This change-round was a relief, as it gave me a chance to recover. I had to make an oblong of dry straw (against the wind), soak it with water, then shake it with the wind into another neat oblong, ready to be drawn out for yelming. You could never shake straw successfully into a stiff breeze. It would come back, wrap itself round your fork and face, and crook the straw till, as Father said, it was 'snarly an' Oi carn't do narthen with it'. Shaking the straw, I kicked in the loose sides, tapped the surface firm with my fork and began to draw out for yelms again.

At long last sister Annie came along the dusty road carrying the old black bag, weighed down with vittles and drink. It seemed quite a time before she stopped in silence before us. 'Put it down on me jacket', Father growled. 'Oi'll ha' me dinner when Oi've done the course.' But before he knocked off he took a drink from the red enamelled tea-can, wiping his mouth on the back of a dark sweaty hand. I was already feeling better with anticipation, being a healthy young animal with vast reserves of energy. Annie whispered that she would ask Father if I could go back home with her, catching him in the right mood over his basin of potatoes, pig's fry and onions. Barely in her teens, she was concerned only with my happiness, remembering her own experience of toil at his hands.

Time seemed to stop as Father struggled into his jacket, took out his old yellowing bone-handled shut-knife, spat on its blade to clean it and lowered himself with a grunt into the dry straw. He apportioned the food, most of it for himself and the rest for me, as Annie had hers at home. She nibbled a straw, watching him unobtrusively from under the brim of her hat, and managed to give me a 'cow's eye' – a wide-open stare which was a deep and secret sign of understanding. Father munched on, tossing me a chunk of bread. I had to pull and gnaw it, not daring to expose a burning secret in my trouser pocket – a shut-knife.

When Annie put it to Father that I should go home with her, he refused. Maybe she should have tapped him before I had had my dinner, so that he could have dismissed me and eaten the lot

Fortunately many of today's thatchers are handing on the tradition. Joseph Stiff of Raydon, Suffolk, shows the way to his son, Russell. (*Tony Ray*)

himself. Anyway, he gathered up the plates and basin into the bag and bade her hurry home. 'An' tell ya mother to git a shirt ready. Oi'm in rags gettin' by they bushes round the back.' Annie made a face behind him, gave me a look of sisterly sympathy and departed the way she had come, turning to wave from time to time till she gradually dissolved into the distance. She was gone; I was alone; the birds stopped singing.

Father settled down to his customary sleep after dinner. His mouth fell open, and in this state of innocent repose he 'drove the pigs to market', as he put it to others who snored. Meanwhile the straw settled under the weight of our bodies with a small whispering sound peaceful as the moment itself. Shifting carefully, I brought out my shut-knife and neatly sliced a few straws diagonally to test its sharpness. I was absorbed in this when the snoring stopped abruptly and Father opened an eye in my direction; he leant over and confiscated the knife. When my disappointment found an outlet in tears, he clumped my head with a tangy paw and fell to appraising the knife for a few moments. Then pocketed it, had a gurgle of tea and set to work again. He knew what was good for me, did Father.

Summer 1961

These Young Men by Martin Sadler

Our main brick chimney-stack needed extensive repairs, and one very hot morning last summer two young men, Jeffrey and Albert, with transistor radio, arrived to erect the scaffolding. It was an intricate job because of the very steep roof and the large flowering shrubs below, but they harmed nothing. On the following day another young man, Colin the foreman mason, appeared, scaled the scaffolding and quickly unpicked the two top courses of weathered bricks.

'Beauties,' he said, 'but what can we do? Can't get bricks like that nowadays. Ordinary one 'ud look cruel'.

When the house was being built nearly forty years ago we found a remarkable man at Rodbourne, near Malmesbury, making sand-faced bricks single-handed. We were allowed to select just what we wanted for two fire-places and two chimney-stacks; and we chose some dark as plums, some greyish and muted, some a pale soft rust. But the brickfield closed down years ago. Now the mortar, made with soft Calne sand, was flaking away in its exposed position at the top of the stack and had caused more damage to the bricks.

'Let's take the van out to Rodbourne and have a look round', urged Albert.

They came back in triumph with three dozen, not from the old brickfield but, at the land agent's suggestion, from the chimney of a derelict cottage near the site.

Colin went up to put them in place, but was soon down again asking me to come and have a look. Alas, these bricks were $3\frac{1}{2}$ in. thick instead of 2 in.; they looked clumsy and top-heavy. I would not have liked to say so after all their trouble in finding them, but Colin took the initiative.

'Won't do', he said. 'Can't have it like that.'

'Well, we've got the electric', shouted Jeffrey; and he plugged a cable into the greenhouse and trailed it through the garden out on to the common, where he spent the day in a temperature of 100° F. and a cloud of orange-pink dust, grinding down the beautiful bricks to the correct thickness. It was marvellous to watch, next morning, the absolute approval of Jim the builder, Colin, Jeffrey, Albert and also Len, the youngest assistant, who

Builders have always found a demand for their skills. (*George H. Hall*)

had come to join them.

Soon Colin came to me again. Did I not think the mortar was drying out too pale? I did, and it was a great pity. He hacked it out and asked me to go with him in the van to inspect a gate pier he had built a mile or so away; this mortar, he thought, might be better. They tried it that afternoon, decided that the tone was still not dark enough and added black to achieve the perfect result. After that Len was given the crude recipe and, early each morning, carefully mixed enough mortar for the day.

The effect was entirely satisfying. With enormous difficulty and dexterity Colin and the acrobatic Albert swept the roof and cleared the guttering, removed the scaffolding – not without some hair-raising moments – cleaned their tools, as they did daily till they shone like new, and left everything shipshape. A few tiles had been damaged but were immediately replaced. Then they said goodbye and departed without a backward glance at their beautiful handiwork. Only young sure-footed men could have tackled the job; and craftsmen with forty years' experience could not have done it better.

Winter 1969

Late Lusher   by **Sheila Sutcliffe**

In answer to my summons, a card arrived with the message, 'Will sweep you Thursday. J. Keal, Late Lusher'. The Lusher family were renowned sweeps of several generations' standing in the district, and now it appeared that all had been gathered save this one nephew. On Thursday we had only just started breakfast when a knock called me to the door; there, completely filling the opening, stood Late Lusher. He was at least six feet six inches tall and broadly built to match his height. From under his sooty cap thick wisps of ginger hair protruded; his moustache was of the same shade and mode of growth. Behind him on the path lay a mass of rods, twisted wires and brushes.

As he came into our house he at once lamented that our chimneys were all so short, needing no more than six rods. 'I though you was an Old Rectory', he observed, 'and would need long rods, like Langton 'All. Now there's chimneys for you', and he licked his lips in joyful recollection of their height, their twists and turns, and the skill required to sweep them clean. We felt our position keenly: our chimneys had most certainly let us down.

Before he left, I proffered the usual cup of tea. As he drank it, he recalled some of the chimneys his family had met with in their career. 'Now there was that one of Mr Coppledyke's down at Skegness', he remarked; 'that were a chimney for you. It were a new 'ouse, not long built, but this chimney, it would smoke; so me Uncle Joe, 'e went to sweep it. But 'e couldn't sweep it, so they sent for me Uncle Abe and 'e couldn't sweep it nohow. So they sent for me Uncle Jock, and 'e couldn't do no good neither'. Here he took a deep breath and so did we, for the suspense was becoming unbearable. 'Then', he continued, 'they sent for me Uncle Benjamin, but that weren't no good neither. And then they sent for me' (at last, we thought, at last) 'and I couldn't sweep it. So then they sent for the builder, and 'e 'ad to pull the chimney down'. He left us feeling very grateful for our short, uncomplicated chimneys.

Spring 1956

Gladys, Chimney Sweep   by E.W.

It began during the War, when her brothers were called up and her father broke his leg. For fifteen miles there was no chimney sweep and it was the spring-cleaning season. There really was nothing else to be done, Gladys must help. She began by going to one or two houses quite near her home, and the thing becoming known, she was pestered by the housewives to come to them. She found she could sling the brushes and the sack for the soot on her bicycle, or over her shoulders, as the men did, and that, although she might be less expert than her father, every job she went to she did better. So she made up her mind to continue, especially as her father's leg did not set well, and gave him constant trouble. And one of the brothers did not come back, and the other married a girl in a distant town and started work there. She now has her printed postcards to send making appointments, and her motor bicycle.

October 1930

All or Nothing   Bridget Wastie, Oxfordshire

When a vacuum chimney-cleaner was brought to the village, the event greatly incensed the old sweep who had served the inhabitants for decades and in his spare time obliged by jobbing gardening. To a former customer who inquired why he had not been to do the garden lately he retorted, 'Beggin' yer pardon, ma'am, what I says is, let them 'as 'lectric sweeps find 'lectric gardeners'.

Summer 1954

Fifty Years a Gardener   by W. E. Shewell-Cooper

Dr Shewell-Cooper, MBE, NDH, FRSL, FLS, DLitt, has had over seventy books published, beginning with *The Garden* in 1932. His ABC series on gardening, which reached twenty-two titles, were the basic guides to innumerable ex-servicemen coming fresh to gardening after 1945.

It is impossible to believe that fifty years have passed since I started gardening seriously. I was born a gardener and have never had any other hobby, so my work has been extremely fascinating and never a bother or burden. But what a difference of approach, what amazing changes of methods, what labour-saving schemes have been introduced – and how unfortunate it has been that we, as a nation, have changed from the good old 'dung' days to artificial chemical fertilisers.

I started under a garden foreman in Kent, who was strict but very kind. He taught me how to spur-prune, how to draw-hoe, how to spread dung evenly and how to sharpen a scythe and a sickle. Today spur-pruning has gone by the board. We thin out, we let the trees grow far more naturally – we even leave our leaders long. The draw-hoe has largely given way to a Jalo, or some other mechanical device like a rotary hoe, while I doubt if many gardeners can use a scythe today. They prefer the Flymo.

Those were the days when we spent hours and hours bedding out, and what intricate designs could be worked out by the good head gardener. He could not, of course, use the same design every year unless the master was old-fashioned and did not like any change. So we had to raise the plants in the greenhouse and they took up a lot of room and, of course, there were the different potting composts to make up and what a problem this was! Very often the head gardener would have his own 'patent' mixtures and if you got another job in another garden, you virtually had to start all over again.

For the tropical plants we had to mix loam, peat and leaf mould in equal parts, and for every bushel we added a six-inch potful of silver sand. The peat and loam had to be stacked in the open, not in a dry shed. Loam was procured from an old pasture that had produced a thick close sward – the sand had to be clean and gritty. For the araucarias I was told to mix equal parts of maiden loam and yellow loam with a little sandy peat, while for aspidistras (very popular in those days) the potting compost was loam and peat in equal parts. Azaleas, on the other hand, had to have three parts of old peat, one part maiden loam and one part sand. So I could go on.

Now, of course, thanks to the work of the John Innes Horticultural Institute, we have all discovered that one compost will suit almost all plants in pots; and in the greenhouses of the organic Good Gardeners' Association, a lot of time and labour is saved as a result of using Alex No-Soil composts for all pot plants.

Still lingering in the greenhouse, we notice that there can be an increase in cropping by the use of carbon dioxide. In the good old days, believe it or not, the head gardener would add all the CO_2 necessary by urinating down the path as he made his last rounds before going to bed. The heating was done by large heavy four-inch pipes around the insides of the house, sometimes in parallel pairs. There were large boilers stoked with coke or coal. What a specialised job it was: someone had to do it late at night, as a general rule, raking out the clinkers, putting the coal or coke in the fire absolutely right in the middle. Stoking had to be learned and woe to the gardener who let the fires out, especially in the winter!

Today we have oil – and 'automatic' oil at that. In the 1920s we had to open all our ventilators by hand; today we have automatic ventilation. When I started we had to water all plants by hand; today we have the choice of mists or trickle irrigation – what a blessing these two have been. In fact, today in many greenhouses, there is almost complete automation.

When we propagated plants in the 1920s we had to use what ingenuity we had; now we have hormones, mist propagation and electric undersoil heat. What primitive methods I was taught to use! As far as insect pests were concerned, quassia chips were boiled and a solution prepared – this was very popular, as was the Richards fumigator. This was lit on three successive evenings with tobacco leaf. There was also the dipping tub, in which infested plants could be completely immersed in tobacco water, while in really bad cases, emulsified paraffin and soft soap was used.

In the vegetable garden, I was taught true trenching and bastard trenching, and what a job this was. The dung was preferably horse – though old cow was allowed. It had to be incorporated nine or ten inches down. Composting was unknown, and so were the modern Growmore fertilizers or granular 'complete' artificial feeds. We only knew animal manures plus sulphate of ammonia, superphosphate and sulphate of potash, which we applied in accordance with the wishes of the head gardener or because of certain instructions in a standard work.

Seed was plentiful and very cheap. There were no pelleted seeds, so we always tended to sow rather thickly because we dared not have blanks. It was always possible to thin; there was plenty of labour. Peas were always supported by pea sticks which were obtained from those who worked in forestry. The sticks were usually hazel and it was right to push the sticks in at an angle of forty-five degrees facing north on one side and facing south on the other, for the rows always ran north and south. Today we have to use wire netting and like it.

What trenches we dug for our celery and cardoons. Today you hardly ever see a cardoon while the common green celery is grown without a trench at all. The rhubarb and seakale would be 'forced' early with special forcing pots while bell cloches would be used for lettuces and radishes. Today, the rhubarb is covered with straw or an old upturned box; if a cloche is used, it is probably made of plastic.

I can still remember the leather shoes that I had to put on the pony's hooves when he was to draw the lawn mower, and what excitement there was when we changed to a motor mower and the poor pony was sold – I hope not to the 'knackers'. In those days, we controlled the daisies and clover too with (believe it or not) sulphate of ammonia. We had to apply it by hand by throwing the powder well into the air so that it fell down evenly as a dust and rested on the bigger leaves of the weeds and fell in between the finer leaves of the grasses. We had no MCPA, or any other hormone for that matter, nor did we feel the need of them. Our lawns of the 1920s were just as beautiful, just as perfect and just as effective for tennis, croquet and golf, as they are today. The gardeners of the twenties were craftsmen as well as being artists.

As a pruner, no trained horticulturist in the 1920s would ever have used secateurs. He had his own pruning knife which he kept sharp on a little whetstone that he kept in his pocket. He never used a knife that closed up in a bone handle; his knife was firm on a wooden handle and was kept in a leather sheath which he kept slung on his belt. His knife was like the sword to a knight. He prized it and used it to great effect. Today few gardeners would know how to use a knife, for secateurs are the vogue.

Who in 1927 had even heard of a plastic pot? The only pots we used were made of clay and we loved them. There were no overhead sprinklers that I remember; if we watered with a hose we used a rose on the end or we stuck it through the handle of a fork which we pushed into the soil.

In my days of training I was most impressed by the writings of Walter P. Wright. He must have written some fifty books which sold well – vegetables, fruit, sweet peas, herbaceous borders – he wrote them all. Now I myself have written seventy-two books on gardening. Can I be the Walter P. Wright of the late 1920s? I sit astonished. . . .

As to the well-known firms, where have they gone? Laxton's, for instance, Bunyard's, Clibran's of Altrincham, Barr's of Covent Garden, Dickson's and Robinson's of Manchester with their famous onion seed, H. Scott of South Norwood and Ryder's of St. Albans? They have departed by being swallowed up by bigger firms. With them have gone many varieties of vegetables we loved and swore by – such varieties as the Early Mazagan broad bean, Negro french bean, Victoria kale, Walcheron broccoli, Wroxton brussels sprouts, Long Red Surrey carrot, Wright's Grove white celery, Rochford's Market Favourite cucumber, Ayton Castle leeks, Ohio lettuce, Essex Star peas, the Bishop potato, Hobday's Giant rhubarb, Bides Recruit tomato and Flanders spinach.

To us who gardened at the time, the flavour of those vegetables was superb; and it is only since we of the Good Gardeners' Association have eschewed any chemical fertilizers that we are back again with the vegetables and salads of the right texture and flavour. So we started with dung and the circle has completed its round, for we are now back to dung or compost as it is today.

But the great thing is that we are still keen gardeners and we still enjoy working with the soil, even though in the olden days we bashed it and now we leave it alone.

Odd Recollections

In the 1920s and 30s we always used water at the same temperature as the pots in the garden. The instruction given in a lecture at Wye College was that cold spring water should never be used until it had been exposed to the air and warmed by the sea. Today we use water at any temperature.

We were told as students that young onions are particularly good food for young turkeys for warding off the attacks of cramp which affect them in dry weather.

The vegetable skirret is not known now – the French call it chervis. It has thong-like roots and we used to cook it like salsify.

Our Lord Himself in the New Testament tells us about salt being used on the Holy Land compost heaps, and in the 1920s it was used 'freely sprinkled on any garden rubbish placed in heaps for decay'.

More seaweed was used in the 1920s than now (except in the case of the members of the Good Gardeners' Association). For beet, for instance, we were taught at college, when digging in the autumn, to bury a liberal quantity of seaweed at the bottom of the trench.

Gardeners' wages and costs: I got £2 10s a week in 1920 (and, a garden frame light cost 7s 6d) – today it is £1000 a year at least!

In the 1920s and 30s we always used to speak about square rods; we never hear the term used today.

On looking through my notes as a student at Wye in the 1920s, I read: 'The site for a hedge should be trenched and manured three feet wide and deep.' 'Box edgings to beds are neat and attractive but they are liable to harbour slugs and other vermin.'

A well-known gardening book of the 1920s states: 'Composts may be formed of waste fish, bones, offal, weeds, human manure, road scrapings and leaves, plus a little lime or salt, thrown in an oblong heap. In a year's time there is a good dressing for heavy soils. Human manure from the earthcloset is especially good for onions, celery, leeks, peas, beans, potatoes, roses, fruit trees. Apply in the spring at 1cwt per square yard.'

1920 instructions to test soil for humus: 'Take 1lb of soil, evaporate the moisture in an oven and put the dried soil on a

shovel over a hot fire until it has ceased to give off any smoke.
When cool, reweigh, and the difference in weight will tell you the
proportion of humus the soil contains.' I ask you!

Spring 1977

Sermons in Stones   by R. W. Kettlewell

For years I wanted to build a Cotswold stone wall, and now at
last I have done it – or a good part of it. There is something
fascinating about the mellowness and durability of stone and in
the challenge of trying to recapture what is almost a lost country
art.

I first felt the attraction of handling and using it in our garden
on the lower slopes of Zomba mountain, where the lovely adminis-
trative capital of Nyasaland looks out over the hot African plain.
The whole hillside is studded with outcrops of massive grey
granite boulders, and littered with lesser stones washed down the
mountain in tropical torrents or left exposed when the softer soil
was eroded away. The rocky outcrops help to soften and restrain
the almost overwhelming green of the rainy-season growth; and

Drystone walling is another craft that is kept alive in villages in
stony parts of the country. Mr Willcocks is shown repairing a Cornish
'hedge' near Lostwithiel. (*George H. Hall*)

they provide shaded corners where plants can have some respite from the scorching sun. In this beautiful setting I enjoyed building steps and low walls to contain the terraced borders. Part of the fascination lay in the patient search for stones to fit and lie in comfortable stability; but it was often frustrating work with irregular blocks and lumps of granite. One could scarcely fail to think with envy of the comparatively convenient shapes and sizes of the sedimentary Cotswold stone. Even after making allowances for the natural nostalgia of an exiled Englishman, it seemed much more attractive in every way.

The opportunity to indulge this preference came when we returned from Africa and faced the problem of enclosing the plot of land on which our house was being built in a Cotswold village. Negotiations, with an old friend as intermediary, secured the promise of advice from her husband, a retired waller who had followed in his father's footsteps since the age of eleven. He was a man of few words: 'Oh ah' was all I could get in answer to most of my early questions. But evidently the first task was to make two wooden profiles, shaped as the cross-section of a wall, between which the building lines would be stretched. 'One inch batter on either side for each foot rise' was my instruction.

This done, I had to dig the 'footings', removing turf and top soil down to something solid. Old Jack set up the profiles for a run of seven or eight yards, briefly enunciated three cardinal principles of walling and left me to it. 'One stone on two' was his somewhat enigmatic way of insisting on a proper bond. 'Pin' each stone with chips and bits so that it is firm. 'Keep the middle filled up', again with bits and pieces, to reinforce the two outer faces and save good walling stone. It is astonishing how much filling is needed. Barrow-load after barrow-load of odd bits, builders' waste and neighbours' rubble, were fitted in; there never seemed to be enough.

The day came when my first few yards of half-finished wall were subjected to silent scrutiny and approved. From then on, whenever it was fine, Jack would come out for an hour or two's walling. Helped by his wife, who kept him supplied with pinners and filled up the middle, he went four times as fast as I did. 'Every stone has its place', he would observe as he infallibly

The partly-built wall with one of the 'profiles' (*John Bowers*)

picked the right one, while I tried mine all ways with increasing exasperation, rejected it and chose another. But your eye for a stone improves with practice, and then there were new lessons. It was fascinating to watch Jack break a stone in a dead straight line by gentle taps in the right place with his short-handled walling hammer. 'Makes two out of one' – an important economy when walling stone costs about £1 for a yard run.

For a while I was completely bewildered by the brief injunction to keep the line 'tingled up'. This was effected by propping it up a bit in the middle, to compensate for natural sag or to give the wall an even run over uneven ground. Jack would stand well back to appraise the lie of the land before deciding where, and how much, to tingle up.

It is a good moment when you raise the line the last six or seven inches to the top of the profile to lay the final courses of stone. Your back is straighter, the wall narrower and progress swifter; and there is the satisfaction of another section finished – except for the toppers ('shuckers', they are called locally) which are set on end across the wall to give it the traditional Cotswold cap. In a field wall, of course, they are laid dry; but in a garden they may be set in cement to give a tidier finish and keep out the weather. 'A good dollop of compo' between each shucker was the prescription. Apart from other merits it helped to economise

'Old Jack and his wife walling' (*John Bowers*)

stone, this far outweighing for Jack the extra cost of cement.

So it goes, each new section being bonded into the last; but it is not solely a matter of skill and patience. This I learnt quite by chance one day when, digging out the footings, I unearthed a halfpenny one hundred years old. I reported this interesting find to Jack. He then confessed that he had already secreted a coin or two of this year of grace in the wall to give it that little bit extra which even the best must have for graceful longevity. As a more overt recognition of the year he carved the figures on a block of freestone and set it in the wall. I hoped this also set a seal of his satisfaction on my apprenticeship.

Walling is hard on the hands, and not even Jack's were immune. The constant gripping, lifting, turning and laying of rough stone plays havoc with the fingers of the left hand. The right, wielding the hammer, has an easier time. Gloves afford only passing protection: leather, cloth and rubber alike all wear through at the sensitive spots, and only the gradual toughening of time is effective.

When there's a touch of frost in the stones and they stick to your fingers with a blistering chill, it takes a lot of determination to keep at it. But on a warm autumn day, with the blackbirds wondering whether perhaps it might be the beginning of spring and the country silence broken only by the chink of the hammer, walling is a most satisfying occupation. As the courses rise and an even run of wall develops, with nothing worse than an aching back as the price of your endeavour, the air is full of the feeling that there are indeed 'sermons in stones and good in everything'.

Winter 1963

An Industry Built on Rock by Helen Harris

The production of roofing slates at Collyweston in Northampton-shire is an ancient industry which still relies on natural elements to aid its processes. Only in the more severe winters, with sustained spells of hard frost, can new material be prepared to help meet the surviving demand.

The material involved is not in fact true slate, but a massive fine-grained sandy limestone which occurs locally at the base of the oolitic Lower Lincolnshire Limestone, overlying the Lower Estuarine Series. It is minutely interbedded with clay which causes horizontal division. Working is reputed to date from Roman times, and it is said that in the thirteenth and fourteenth centuries, when the area was afforested, charcoal burners building rough shelters of stone made much use of the outcropping slate for roofing.

The area where the rock is obtained, north of Collyweston village, lies at an altitude of just over 300ft – one of the highest points in the locality. Here, close to the borders of Lincolnshire and with Leicestershire in view, is the 'slaters' drift' where, in the past, numerous men occupied 2-acre plots, farming the land with barley, turnips and sheep, and working the slate, which they extracted in winter, prepared in the spring and used for roofing buildings in the summer.

The quarrying is done in small underground mines at a depth of around 30ft; there is about 10in of topsoil above the main overburden, locally called 'kale', and a thin layer of sand lying immediately above the actual limestone known as Collyweston slate.

In the 1920s there were six slating firms operating at Colly-weston; today there are three who work and use the natural product as the superior material for their trade. One of those still remaining is Mr Bob Osborn, whose family has lived in the parish and been connected with the work for over 350 years, and who, with his foreman, Mr Stan Harrod, has been in the business for fifty years. His working, which has been in use for 200 years at least, is entered drift-wise from the floor of an old quarry, and extends horizontally underground 30–40yds. Height in the passages between the face and the back-filled, previously-worked area is about 5ft, but headroom is low, starting from nothing in the section being undermined. The passages are winding and the working sections irregular, due to variations in the rock; in places the limestone exhibits a vertical fissure, known as a 'dry face' to the slaters, who consider the cleft an advantage and work towards it. The activity is often referred to as 'foxing' or 'going down a foxhole', and the chief tool used, consisting of a small sharpened single-ended pick on a wooden handle, is called a foxing pick.

Slate is extracted when there seems a likelihood of several days of hard freezing conditions. With candles – or perhaps the refinement of a pressure lantern – for lighting, and a straw-filled sack on which he lies, the worker picks away at the sand and rock beneath the layer of sought-after limestone for a distance of about 12–14ft, across a width of a few feet depending on the nature of the rock. Stone pillars of blue rag ('blue bastard') surmounted by pieces of slate are built up as supports. From time to time as he proceeds the worker gently taps the rock close above his head in several places, gauging from the sound whether or not it is safe to continue. Warning of the ceiling's impending settling is heard as a series of little clicks – 'talking' as it is known. Then it is time to retreat; with the pieces of slate on top of the pillars probably already cracking the pillars are knocked out, and, with a thunderous crash, as much as 200 tons descends.

Sometimes, however, the limestone will not immediately drop even when the supports are removed. Ideally the 'drop' stage is at the end of the day's work when, if it does not come at once, the men may leave and hope to find the fall awaiting them the next morning. In some instances it is necessary to help the process, which is done by what is termed 'ravage amusement'; steel wedges are driven in at ceiling level, and a bar of iron, called a 'lion's tail', is used to wedge and lever away the ceiling.

The material from Mr Osborn's working is raised from the entrance to ground level by means of a motor hoist and scaffolding, but within living memory a hand windlass was employed, while some pits used a horse and small cart. On the surface the 'green' slabs are laid out like crazy paving and kept wet. It is important to retain the stone's natural 'sap' so that the action of the frost can initiate splitting; if the stone is allowed to dry out and re-wetted artificially the same effect can never be achieved, since subsequent freezing will be only superficial. The slates are split down to a thickness of $\frac{1}{4}$–$\frac{3}{8}$in by the skilful use of a cliving hammer, which, if the frost has done its work, appears to ease rather than force them apart.

The irregularly-shaped slates are then worked to precise dimensions with a dual-headed dressing hammer; they are first dressed to approximate shape with the flat, 'batten' side, after which the claw side is used to nip off unwanted pieces. Holes to enable the slates to be hung – nowadays usually by nails, but formerly by wooden pegs – are then made. Though the modern way of doing this is with an electric drill the craftsman's method still survives at Collyweston, for which a 'bill', a tool made from a metal file mounted in a boxwood bill helve, is employed. First a very ancient process called 'splashing' is carried out, involving hitting the slate with the bill at an angle, until a small piece of slate shoots out leaving a shallow depression, in which the actual hole is then made by 'riming' – screwing it with the point of the bill until a regular hole of the required size is obtained. To save their hands on this job Mr Osborn and his foreman have devised protectors of folded leather with rings cut to fit over fingers and thumbs.

The slates are then 'parted up' and arranged in groups according to size, from the larger pieces – 2ft or more in length – for the lower sections of roofs, to 6in pieces for use at ridge level. Long-established names are used to denote different lengths of slate on a scale from 6in to 2ft, which aspiring slaters learned to recite along the wooden rule, lineated in half-inches, at an early age. Slates less than 6in long are described as Out-rule, and the others, some of which are subdivided, in ascent as: Mopes; Mumfats; Jobs; Short ones; Long ones; Short, Middle and Long backs; Bachelors; Whibbits; Twelves; Fourteens; Sixteens; Eighteens; Imbows; Outbows; Short, Middle and Long tens.

The other two slate mines still open at Collyweston, situated close to Mr Osborn's, are those of Mr R. J. Spall and Messrs J. W. Stapleton & Sons. Mr Spall's, which is entered similarly to that of Mr Osborn, is the largest and involves an area of eleven acres, of which only about three acres have been worked out, so there are considerable reserves; no fresh slate has been extracted here, however, for the past ten years, as a result mainly of the succession of mild winters. The Stapletons' mine differs from the other two in having, for access, a 35ft vertical shaft.

Collyweston slates, which are harder and thinner than those that have been worked in other areas of the Oolite, are lighter in weight per square foot than modern concrete tiles, and, not surprisingly, cost two-and-a half times as much. (They are, however, still cheaper than slates from Cumbria and from Delabole in Cornwall.) Used for centuries in the village and in much of the district around on houses constructed of the honey-grey local stone, they have also been employed much farther afield; colleges at Oxford (including Somerville and Nuffield) and at Cambridge have Collyweston slates in their roofs, as also have a building near Land's End and a shooting lodge near Wick in Scotland, and they were used in 1955 for the restoration of London's Guildhall. The lodge at Wick was roofed by Mr Osborn's father who in 1906 also travelled with another man to America, to use his slates in roofing a mansion being built from all-British materials on Long Island for a Mr Phipps, partner of Andrew Carnegie the Scottish philanthropist.

The pleasing aesthetic effect of the use of Collyweston slate is unquestioned. Today, though for economic reasons the demand is diminished, orders are still received from people who want no other roofing material, and the Collyweston slaters receive many more enquiries than they can satisfy. A number of these come from the Cotswold area, where the Stonesfield quarry near Oxford – formerly an important source of roofing slate – and others have gone out of production, and where there are very few slaters remaining with the skill necessary for working the natural material.

At Collyweston, as also in the Cotswolds, much work is done with old slates which have been in use for up to 600 years. They are brought to the works, cleaned and reconditioned, and are then, in the words of Bob Osborn, 'given a breath of Collyweston air, as good as new'. Since the craft still survives here and as there are ample reserves, it could be that Collyweston offers the only future supply of natural roofing material of the type traditional throughout the Wolds, provided of course, that adequate labour with the necessary skill for extraction and preparation can be maintained, and that there are convenient recurrences of that other essential factor for winning new material – extreme winter frost.

Autumn 1975

Millwright's Craft   by Edward Whitney

Our water-mill was built beside a small river in Cambridgeshire, and we were responsible for the upkeep of some two miles of river bank. In winter and early spring, when the river became swollen after heavy rains and snow, we had to keep a vigilant eye on the banks, for if the water were to break through, great damage would be done to land most of which was arable. We also had to keep the river clean of the rushes and other weeds which grew in profusion. These were cut during the summer. Six to eight five-foot knives, shaped like those of a farm mowing-machine, were bolted loosely together end to end, and a piece of rope was tied to each outside knife. We worked steadily up river, a man on each bank, pulling the knives slowly from side to side along the bed in a sawing motion. As the rushes and weeds were cut they bobbed to the surface and floated gently downstream, until they were caught against the sluice-gate. There they were raked out and left to dry on the bank.

We had an old millwright named Roger Rayment, who was nearly eighty years old and wore a skull-cap when working. Never do I hope to see a better craftsman. Whatever job he undertook was done well and to last, whether it was the replacing and fitting of spouting or floors, or the setting of heavy mill machinery. It was he who dressed the millstones, which were made of French burr, the hardest stone obtainable, and were about four feet in

There are few millwrights left; Mr Heasmen of Coltsford Mill in Surrey carries on the precise craft of dressing millstones. (*R. E. Balch*)

diameter. The method of dressing varied. The grooves did not radiate from the centre, but were set out at a tangent to the drift circle, as shown in the accompanying diagram. The main grooves or master furrows varied in number with the 'quarters' into which the surface of the stone was divided. The smaller grooves intersecting each of the quarters were termed secondary furrows. The top surface of the stone between the furrows was called the 'land'

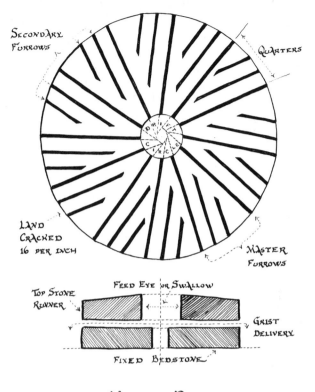

Millstone dress (*Edward Whitney*)

and was usually 'cracked' or 'snecked' about sixteen grooves per inch to give the maximum grinding power.

The functions of the furrows were threefold: to distribute the wheat and meal over the grinding surface, to partly reduce the grain, and to supply air for ventilation to keep the grinding surfaces cool. The grinding action was obtained by fixing one stone and revolving a second against it. General practice favoured fixing the bottom or bed-stone and rotating the other, called the top-stone runner. The stones were supported on either a floor or a special iron or timber husting.

The wheat was shovelled into the 'eye' of the stone by a shaker or joggle-feed and, getting into the furrows, was dragged between the lands in widening circles, until it finally fell out round the circumference of the stones in the form of meal. The centrifugal action of the revolving stone helped the grain on its outward journey. Unless the stones were carefully dressed and run truly with a good even feed, the stock or grist would be found to be heated as it was discharged. If the feed were taken off the stones while they were set close for heavy grinding, the surfaces would become 'bottle-faced', that is, blunted. Then the stones could not be dressed again and were useless.

A water-wheel about twelve feet in diameter turned the stones, its only disadvantage being that the drive was sometimes uneven. As we maintained the banks we had the use of the water free, after we had paid tithe to the parson.

Autumn 1952

Welsh Miller   by P.G.

His old grey mill had been worked by his father and by his grandfather before him, in the little Welsh mountain village clustered round the tiny grey church from which it takes its name of Chapel of the Red-haired Princess. The miller, a delightful raconteur, talks as he works. A few years ago he took to playing the violin. He practises in the mill, his only audience a white cat which goes with him everywhere.

Plump pigs and thriving hens are always part of the stock-in-trade of the old tolling mills. Millers in these parts still exact toll in lieu of cash payment for grinding corn. That is, they keep back a percentage of grain from every sack for their own use; hence the pigs and hens. (Under an old law a miller was forbidden to keep more than three hens and a cock.) The grain is extracted in a wooden peck measure, bound with iron bands and shiny with use. I watched the miller carry a measure of grain and empty it into his old oak grain-chest. 'Father used to say no miller got his full share; he has to put his two thumbs into the measure to lift it!' He was half-way up the stairs as he said this to take a full sack from where it hung by a strong steel cable forged long ago in the village. He swung the sack deftly to the edge of a hopper, and unhooked the chain. He could handle hundredweights of corn as a grocer handles pounds of sugar. 'Father could always tell if the casual labourers who wanted to dress the stones were really used to mill work or not', he said, as he poured the wheat into the wide mouth of the hopper. 'He just put them to lift a sack off the chain as it travelled up, like I did now, and if they weren't used to it they couldn't judge the weight of the sack and the speed it was travelling, and they always missed it.

'Nowadays I have to dress the stones, especially the wheat stones, myself', he went on. The difficulty of getting men to do the dressing has led some millers to use their wheat stones for barley and for coarse meal for animals. This has ruined the stones, and when they are used again for wheat there are complaints of the flour being coarse and gritty. But there are, I need hardly say, millers who can produce flour like silk, with a pleasing texture.

My miller frequently goes off to give a hand in the harvest fields. It pays him to be well acquainted with his customers, and to know their crops. 'I've never seen so much wheat grown round here', he said, 'and the first thing the farmers want is for me to grind some to take back to their wives to bake wholemeal bread in the brick ovens, same as they got as boys.'

'Does English wheat make good bread?' I asked. 'Sweetest flavour in the world', he said, and plunged his hand into a heap of amber grain. 'Now this is April Bearded, one of the best kinds for this locality, and this one is Red Marvel, which is nearly as good. Of course it isn't hard and tough like the wheat from parched prairie lands, the kind that's been so popular with the milling trade latterly because of the way it absorbs moisture in the washing process. English wheat is soft and contains so much natural moisture it won't take up water. It's profitable, of course, selling water, and this has been the cause of a lot of complaint against wholemeal not keeping. You see, when the germ's wet it ferments, but if the wheat is cleaned dry the way we do it, it'll keep well enough. Of course the quality and the flavour of wheat differs according to where it's grown. What I buy from the market up in the hill country doesn't compare for bread with what's grown on land down there by the river. And you have to be very careful of autumn frosts with wheat. In the old days, when the harvests were late, we used to have to eat bara mall (bread made from flour with a disease known as "rope"). The crust'd look all right, but the inside of the loaf'd be all wet and sticky, and have a sickly smell of yeast.' 'Why don't we get it now?' 'Nowadays farmers all use so much artificials, the crops come earlier. Why, when I was a child the corn off the fryddoel [uplands] was never cut before about October 21; now they cut and cart it before October. Of course it does still break out in the bakeries sometimes, but I'm told the bakers counteract it by adding certain chemicals to the dough.'

The old Welsh mills have kilns for producing oatmeal. In the houses it is good to see the barley loaves and oatcakes rolled out thin, and baked, as large as dinner plates, on a girdle, and to see them hung up in a special wooden receptacle on a kitchen beam, to be kept for making 'shot', the traditional dish of crushed oatcake and buttermilk which in summer always replaced the winter porridge as the first dish at supper-time.

The talk at my miller's fireside fell upon old preachers. 'Some of them would go up into the pulpit in the brown corduroys and clogs of the Welsh labourer, but I remember one old man was all dressed up in a frock coat and starched cuffs. When he got well into his "hwyl" he made a sweeping gesture with his right arm. Away sailed the cuff up into the gallery. Not at all taken aback he made a similar gesture with his left, and away sailed the other. "That one can go too!" he cried; "they wouldn't have been there anyway if it hadn't been for Mary!" '

October 1941

Sawing was Thirsty Work   by Thomas Hudson

I was making a set of chairs and needed to trim some pieces of oak to length for the back splats. I reached for the saw, made the necessary cuts and replaced it. One small operation in the midst of many. Normally I would not remember having done it, so much do I take the saw's use for granted. Only if it needs sharpening do I make any mental note of it, for I expect it to perform always without fault. This is true, of course, of many tools, and one pays tribute to all those who have developed and perfected their use over the years. As I replaced the saw this time I stopped, lifted it down again and looked at it, seeing it properly as the modern descendant of those flint, copper and early iron saws which must have been sheer misery to use. I felt the wood handle, tapped the steel blade, and ran my eye down the straight sharp row of teeth. I noted, with satisfaction, how each tooth was set alternately sideways to ensure cutting a wider cut or 'kerf' than the rest of the blade, to prevent the saw pinching in the wood. As I held it in sawing position and appreciated its balance, I wondered what the old woodworkers before the age of tempered steel would have thought of it, or even those famous furniture makers of the seventeenth century.

I use twelve different woodsaws in my workshop and would miss any one of them, but the heavy sawing of trees and the conversion of timber ready for seasoning is done today by machine in the saw mill. This has only developed during living memory, and timber was still sometimes converted by hand at the end of the last war.

When horse and man were the only sources of power, timber was felled in the dead of winter when the sap was down. Carpenters and wheelwrights would buy it standing and have to fell as well as cart it home. Only by levering and the use of pulleys and horse were the great logs manoeuvred first on to the long timber carriage or pole wagon and then over the saw pit. A tool known as a 'ring-dog' was much used for levering, and was one of those simple but highly effective pieces of equipment that our forefathers were so adept at devising.

Sawing trees into usable timber without a mechanical saw was done over a saw pit, a rectangular hole dug in the ground with perhaps a few boards wedged in the ends to keep the earth from falling in, and two stout beams running along the sides at the top which bore the cross beams. These cross beams supported the log to be sawn and needed to be straight-grained and strong enough to avoid the log falling into the pit, crushing the bottom sawyer who operated from underneath. Apart from this hazard, a heavy log which had fallen into the pit was a problem to remove as well as a waste of time. The log was held securely by 'iron dogs' driven into the beams as well as into the log itself. When a chalk line had been marked for guidance, the top of the log often being trimmed first so that the line could be seen more easily, the sawing proceeded. The top sawyer held the long pit saw with the 'tiller' or top handle and guided the cut along the line, while the bottom or pit sawyer, poor fellow, gave power to the other end down in the pit. He suffered a continuous shower of sawdust which clung to his sweating body and got in his eyes if he looked up at the wrong moment. The pit was damp and dark and his hands, through constant use, polished the handles of the 'box' or bottom handle. The box was held to the saw blade by a simple wedge, so that it was quickly removed to enable the saw to be withdrawn from the cut when a beam was reached. The log was then moved along by levering one of the cross beams round after removing the iron dogs. This beam, known as the 'pit-roll', was round in section, and had holes in each end: a bar was inserted in one end to lever it.

Apparently pit sawing was only common in England and Denmark, and elsewhere it was usual to carry out the same process above the ground with the log supported by trestles. The term pit-saw is replaced by such names as 'long' or 'length' or 'cleaving saw', referring to the same tool in other countries.

Sawyers had a reputation for being great drinkers and are said to have spent much of their spare time in pubs. Nevertheless, they were undoubtedly men of skill and certainly they needed to follow a straight line without deviation on returning from slaking their sawdusty thirst. It was tedious work: Walter Rose, writing of sawyers in 1937, said that 'The monotonous slog . . . tended to develop a dumb mentality' and added, 'I have never met a sawyer who has expressed regret at the passing of the work over to the machine.'

When sawing was all done by hand a man never sawed along the grain if he could cleave it; for example, chair rails were always riven from the log. Riven wood is stronger than sawn wood as the latter ignores the grain. There used to be a saw-pit close to where I live, just inside an estate yard at Odell, Bedfordshire. There is no trace of it now, but recently a big circular saw formerly used in the woods was moved from where it had stood idle for years to the site of the old saw pit. It is very rusty but a glance reveals it as a powerful successor to the pit-saw, although the earliest circular saws could only handle logs which had first been pit-sawn. I understand that timber was sawn by water power here at the mill in the village during the last war.

A saw that has gained in popularity over the last few years for rough sawing of green timber is the tubular frame or bushman's saw, often wrongly called a bowsaw. I find it difficult to convince people that I occasionally enjoy a little rough sawing, but not long ago a farmer friend called to offer me some boughs that had fallen from an ash into one of his fields. It needed sawing up and fetching. Having no chain saw I took the bushman's along with an axe to convert some quite sizeable pieces into firewood. The day was perfect for the task, bright, sunny, but with a definite nip in the air. Although there was a considerable amount to get through, by the end of the afternoon all the timber was stacked in convenient lengths ready to carry home, and I looked appreciatively again at the simple modern saw which I know would have astounded woodcutters of the past.

Spring 1974

A Trio of Blacksmiths   **by Frank Boughton**

Since our daughter Betty decided to dedicate most of her waking and dreaming life to ponies and the pony club, my wife and I have had many strange and interesting experiences. Of our new acquaintances perhaps the trio of blacksmiths are the most memorable. Of course, a smith is like any country expert – builder, joiner, plumber, mechanic – in being independent and self-reliant, with a stubborn pride in his skill and the worth of his trade. In no country workshop is the customer always right, and he will certainly be told when he is not. But other trades seem to belong to this age – the car mechanic is a creature of it – in a way that the shoeing smith does not. His is a blunt, tough, dangerous trade. One smith I know limps from a damaged hip, another is racked by headaches from a fractured skull, and a third has forearms flecked with scars left by countless nail-points.

Most country craftsmen have the habit of criticising their trade rivals with great freedom. Gouging and hacking off slabs of crumbling plaster or dry-rotted wood, the builder tuts complacently and says: 'Gone! All gone, see. Rotten as a pear. Who put this lot in, then?' Smiths take this kind of thing even farther. Half of their conversation consists of what the advertising business would call 'knocking copy'. A new smith saunters into your shed,

Although in the days of horse transport every village had its forge and farrier, today's blacksmiths are more often occupied in making decorative wrought ironwork. (*J. A. M. Kreyer*)

puts down his tool-box, picks up a hoof and delivers a detailed analysis of the faults in the last shoeing. While he is operating, his anecdotes illustrate the incredible incompetence, negligence and cowardice of all other smiths within a ten-mile radius.

As pony-owners we came into contact first with Ben who at seventy-nine years of age was, not surprisingly, in the twilight of his smithing career. We struck the problem of his independence early on. He came to his cottage door, his big shoulders drooping now, long brown scarred arms hanging ape-like, his eyes still bright, mischievous, fierce. His wife was visible in the shadows behind him and gave tongue the instant the door opened: 'Don't you leave my dog go in the road.'

'I've shut the gate. Can you shoe the pony, Ben?'

'When?'

'Saturday?'

'Not if you comes late. I likes the wrestling, so I aren't missing that.'

'Suppose we brought her down half-past two?'

'Ay,' he said rather grudgingly, 'so long as it's not after.'

The missis spoke again: 'And he likes "Tarzan" too, so it's no good you coming at five.'

Looking back on our time with Ben, I recall a constant atmosphere of drama. That first shoeing was a dramatic affair. Our pony is a sturdy thirteen-hand mare not in her first youth; she had not long before been pricked pretty painfully by a smith some way off, and had not forgotten. In my memory now it is all a sweaty ill-tempered ballet: the matronly mare rearing like a colt, Ben cursing and jumping and shouting, Betty leaping on and over piles of junk around the walls to avoid the flying hooves, Ben's tool-box receiving a full-blooded kick and disintegrating in a cloud of dust, rust and old nails. 'By God, mare, you've a-come to the wrong house to play', said Ben, jabbing her hard between the ribs with the shaft of his hammer; whereupon the mare demonstrated that so far she had indeed been merely playing at being awkward.

At the end of an eventful ninety minutes Ben watched from the forge door, as Betty trotted the mare up and down the lane: 'That old bay have a-gone real wicked. Used to be so quiet as a babby. Shoe'd her many a time, I did, when she was over at Cold Blow. Perhaps it's the forge she don't like.'

We had no more set-outs like that, but the same air of drama pervaded Ben's shoeing stories. He had several gypsy clients, and they were the main source of excitement. 'Had a mule in, Monday. Gippo brought 'un in. Well, there was a bliddy kicker, mun. Front feet, back feet – nearly got me with a cow-kick. "No good," I said, "on'y one thing to do – rope the bogger up." So we tied one foot fast of another and threw 'un. Missis was screaming at me all the time to let 'un alone. Anyhow we piled 'un down on the floor, an' I shoe'd 'un with his feet up in the air. Well, good God, there was a row: gippo cursing him up in a heap, mule shouting, the missis shouting. Drop dead if I know which was the worst.'

We passed from Ben to Ted in a characteristically abrasive way, with every stage attended by the greatest ill-will. Ben's missis, very much an *éminence grise* in that household, decided on rather slender evidence that our pony was too dangerous for her man to shoe, and we had perforce to transfer to Ted a few miles off.

'Ay, ay,' said Ted when I approached him, 'I'll shoe her for
thee. And don't worry about old Ben; 'a won't put me off. Good
God, that old bay aren't dangerous. I knows her. I shoe'd 'un a
colt. Just a bliddy yarn of old Ben's, boy.'

The next time I saw Ted I had something for him: 'I've got
that set of old shoes for the mare from Ben. You wanted them for
size. They look a bit big to me.'

I handed him a heavy front shoe about a foot across. He
looked at it and spat in disgust, then turned red with rage and
was seized by a paroxysm of wheezing and coughing: 'I don't
know, drop squint I don't, how that old devil is so wicked to me.
That's never in this world her size. I knows her, see. Shoe'd 'un
a colt. He's hoping I'll set to and make a set of shoes all wrong. I
knows 'un. 'A stopped me in the mart t'other day and says to me
I'm taking the bread from his mouth. "You've a-come to my very
door, boy," he says, "to take my customers off me." "Look, Ben,"
I says, "how are you talking so bliddy dull, boy? You failed on the
mare and sent her from you. Fair play," I says, "Mr Boughton
had to find someone else." "She've gone too dangerous to get
under", he says. Anything, he'll say, to put me off. But I told him
I used to shoe her a colt, just fast of a ring in that wall by there.
No-one to help. The li'l maid that had her would work the forge
for me.'

During the past two years Ted has turned up regularly in his
van, arriving always on a day and at a time fixed by him. He
unloads his gear with much clanking and jingling and comes into
the shed, his short stout body rolling, a Woodbine in his mouth.
His face is palish, glistening, sprouting hairs; his thick serge
waistcoat and blue ex-railway trousers meet at an ample convex
equator formed by a thick brass-buckled leather belt. His very
flat and limp cloth cap is removed, tilted, replaced or pushed
back to mark the rhetorical flourishes of his narratives, which
usually begin as he enters the shed and continue sporadically.
Luckily for the mare, he is better disposed towards her than
to his trade rivals; he is calm and slow, kind and deliberate with
her, picking up her feet in turn, keeping up a flow of crooning
horse-chat: 'Come on then – hup! Hup, will you, maid? Hold
still there – woop'ta – stand then. How're you so bliddy nasty to

me t'day, maid? – Hold still then, or it's the twitch for you, my lady – shan't give thee a sweet nor nothing.' All these threats are delivered in a soothing monotone.

In between shoeing the feet Ted rests an arm comfortably on the mare's broad rump and philosophises about life as he sees it: 'You know old Flatt? Lives in town. Keeps a couple of ponies. Come out t'me th'other night: would I shoe a colt? I says okay – done her last Monda' week. Hell of a job with 'un – kick, bite, rear, everything. You know what I found after?' His cap was flipped back, then pulled down in front again as he glowered red and bristling at the duplicity of man: 'I found 'a'd had Ben and young Bob at the colt, and they'd booth failed on 'un. Then he gets me in there and never lets on about the others. "Well, Flatt," I says, "seeing as you never let me know them others had failed on 'un, I aren't charging you the usual, I'm charging you a bliddy fiver. And", I says, "I'll tell ye something else: ye're nothing else but a dirty bogger." ' He spat with great emphasis among the grey-blue hoof-parings and seized another foot. 'So I aren't driving another nail for him.'

He works on, sweating and wheezing in the close shed, cutting and shaping, nailing and clenching. When the last foot has been clenched down and rasped off smooth, he straightens with a snort, drops his tools in the box and begins to fumble in the left pocket of his distended waistcoat. The mare, who knows him of old, swings her head round, the eye-whites gleaming in the gloom. 'Been a good old maid t'day', he says, and produces a small brown virulently strong cough-sweet. The pony draws it up eagerly out of his hand and eats it.

We met Jim, doyen of his profession and still shoeing hard at eighty-one, when Ted was ill. After a lot of delicate negotiation, it was settled that we would buy the set of shoes Ted had made, and get Jim to put them on. Betty and I walked the pony over, six or seven miles through a maze of winding lanes, till we came out at last on to the bare moor near the sea, and soon saw the thin gaunt tin chimney of Jim's forge sticking up from a dense huddle of bushy willows.

I had been told that old Jim was very deaf; he was clinking away with a big hammer at some wrought-iron gates, and it was our shadows in the doorway that attracted his attention. He seemed a frail old man for a shoeing smith – tall, but lean and stooping, his arms stringy with tendon and muscle. He limped from the hip after a vicious kick which had all but got him down a year ago. But this frailty was belied by the way those lean arms opened out into huge confident brown hands, and by the quick vital rhythm of his hammering.

When we had blinked our eyes into vision in the gloom we saw the dull red-eyed glow of the fire, the vast dusty ashy jumble of old iron about the walls; the cold daylight coming through the open top half of the door fell on a polished hollow in the dry beaten earth floor, the hollow where for fifty years pony and donkey, cob, hunter and cart-horse had stood to be shod, each of those ten thousand hooves turned up and back to catch that struggling light.

Old Jim walked across with the slow crippled dignity of a stork, laid an all-wise hand on the mare's back and looked critically at her feet. 'Ted's shoeing? Thought so. Too short in the toe, all his work. Put on cold? Rough job, that. These the shoes to go on? Says he made 'em? Ready-made, these are; bought stuff. Look at these back shoes: both the same. Shouldn't be like that.' And with the slightest twitch of his wrist he sent the four heavy shoes whizzing across the forge on to a great pile of old ones.

Moving with that deceptively slow stalk about the pony, he knocked up the clenches and tugged off the old shoes, grunting, blowing and spitting with the effort. He pared long shavings of horny blue hoof from her feet and clipped out a 'V' in front of each hoof to fit the raised toe of the shoe. Then began the long finicking job of fitting each shoe exactly to each foot, and I saw why many owners of the best horses in the district came for miles for his shoeing. Over and over again he would toss a shoe into the dull crimson dust of the fire, pump the bellows until coal and shoes were a blazing lightish red, then put one shoe on the anvil and hammer it with that same almost frenzied rhythm, twisting and turning it deftly with the tongs, sending flakes and sparks of red-hot metal in arcs to the floor. In between blows on the shoe he would rap the anvil to keep up the driving pace of his hammer. Then he would knock the tang of a rasp into a nail-hole, limp across and try the shoe on the foot; strings and coils of acrid grey smoke came from the burnt hoof, making the pony blow and snort. If the fit was a millimetre out, back into the forge with the shoe, and it all started again.

Jim too talked as he worked: 'Got a bad kick up here in the hip a year or so back. Bliddy horse cow-kicked me. Took best part of a year to get back here. I'm all right now. Did three hunters yesterday. "Retire", they said. But I says, "What would I do if I retired?" '

At last he finished, and before we left he dashed oil on the mare's beautifully shod feet, so that they gleamed in the sun. 'There y'are then. I s'pose they'll be all wrong to Ted when he sees 'em. He'll never give me a good word, I know. Here's his shoes back; no use to me.' And without any apparent difficulty he retrieved the rejected shoes from the pile.

'You're wrong in one way about Ted', I said, as I led the pony into daylight again. 'He kept on about what a good tradesman you were. He admires your work a lot.'

The old man stood in the forge door silent and nonplussed, almost as if betrayed. Without a word he half-lifted his hand in a farewell, then turned and was lost in the black gloom.

Summer 1971

Jones and Son   by A. M. Dutton

Twenty years ago I was a vicar in a Leicestershire parish where the smithy was a busy place. The blacksmith, Thomas Jones, aged seventy-eight, was assisted by his son, a mere youngster of fifty. The old man was a devout churchman, with a splendid tenor voice and a whole host of anecdotes which would be punctuated by the blows from his hammer.

One day I broke a tine of my gardening fork and, knowing that old Thomas sold new tools – an innovation of his son's – I went round to the smithy. 'Why buy a new un?' demanded the old man indignantly. 'Bring un along.' I did, and he mended it so that I could hardly see where the tine was welded. I still have that fork. The job cost ninepence. On another occasion new fire bars were needed for the church boiler and were going to cost more than £5. I went round to old Jones. Yes, he could make a new set.

Then and Now   by Brian Walker

'The smith a mighty man is he . . .'

Spring 1977

The cost would be fifteen shillings but, as it was for the church, there would be no charge. They were a good set of bars, too.

It was the old man, oddly enough, who sounded his own death-knell. He took me to the back of the forge to point out the small electric blower that was replacing the old-fashioned hand-bellows. 'Goin' to be pretty useful', he said. Then the son began to take time off to attend courses at the technical school in the near-by market town. He was studying oxy-acetylene and electric welding as well as agricultural engineering. When the oxygen cylinders appeared in the smithy, the old man eyed them with suspicion but carried on with his work.

With the rapid mechanisation of agriculture after the war, young Jones found his newly acquired knowledge of great use, and we began to realise that he had brains as well as brawn. His father soon had little to do but shoe a few horses; even these became steadily less numerous. I think he realised that the old regime was ending when an apprentice arrived in the smithy. With more machinery repairs young Jones needed a little help. The old man was practically speechless when he found that the terms of apprenticeship laid down shorter hours for the lad, and that he was to be given one full day's leave each week to attend the technical school. 'I never 'ad to go to school to learn my trade', muttered old Jones. 'My father taught me, an' 'is father taught 'im. As for hours, five till eight 'twas for me, an' five till four Saturdays.'

It was not long before we missed seeing the tall well-built figure going to work in the smithy. The old man was approaching his eightieth birthday, and the weight of years, together with a feeling that he was unwanted in his modernised smithy, began to tell on him. For a few weeks he pottered about the house; but he soon took to his bed, where I visited him regularly until he died a few months later.

Yesterday I passed the old smithy. It has become a hive of industry. A few horses, chiefly hunters, are still shod there, but only to oblige farmers who bring their other work.

Spring 1965

Plumber to Trade   by Humphrey Drummond

The notice fixed to Duncan Fraser's street window read, ASER ND ONS UMBERS, and it was the more difficult to read as it had slipped crookedly across the panes. I asked the old man what had happened to his sons.

'Oh, they all went off, like young people do. There's only me now, and I can't get about like I used. Look at me warehouse', he added, pulling me by the sleeve and pressing me against a hole in the corrugated iron partition. 'There's me stock, but I can't get it shifted.'

'You mean you haven't the key on you?'

The handsome ancient face creased appreciatively. 'Not got me key on me! No, nor had it this while past. Not since that traveller came. I mind the day clear enough. A great big old brown horse he had between the shafts, and a wall eye. The horse I mean. I got some fine suites in there, for sure, but of course I haven't looked them over just recent.'

My hope of persuading Duncan to instal the plumbing in my reconstructed cottage took a steep downward curve. 'Can we not get into the store through a window?' I suggested.

'That's an idea that's come to me many a time. I'm not such a fool as I look, you know. But you've got one drawback to yer plan. There's no window.'

'What about changing the lock then?'

'Once you get chaps changing locks all over the place, you don't know where it's going to end', he objected. 'But where there's a will there's a way, as my old father used to tell us boys. Never at a loss was me dad. He'd 'a' thought up something quick, like lifting the door off its hinges.'

'Well, how about trying that?' I ventured, not very hopefully. It must have been some decades since Duncan had been able to inspect his stock, and he might have forgotten how to do plumbing.

'We could.' He was quite taken with the idea, nodding approval and encouragement as I gently lifted the door from the sagging rusted hinges. Inside stood a number of dust-laden humps of straw. Duncan moved from shape to shape, his fingers scrabbling eagerly with the packing. Presently he stooped to the floor and picked up a stock card, and after a moment found the catalogue from which the stock had been ordered.

'Now I can let you know what I've got for you', he said briskly. 'There's a complete Marlborough, left or right delivery, with vitreous pan, or an Imperial centre flush, bronze release extra. Supplies of the new Wimpole modification subject to delay . . . Any of these straight from stock. I'll get me nephew down and start this week.'

I chose a Devonshire with centre flush. The bath had dragon's feet and fancy soap-tray. Although the smallest of five at the back of the store, it looked as if it would hold about a hundred gallons. The taps were more like stopcocks for a fire hydrant. For a wash-basin I had a choice of pillar, bracket or wall model, 'each tastefully decorated in contemporary style', as Duncan put it. The wall model, a riot of Michaelmas daisies under the shining glaze, was nice but out of the question; it must have weighed several hundredweight and would have brought my little house down round my ears. The pillar model, I feared, would go through the floor, and the bracket model with vast wrought-iron supports would destroy both floor and wall.

But Duncan had now taken complete control. My objections were swept aside, the work put in hand. I still don't know how he managed it, but my bathroom with fittings is now one of the wonders of the village, even if I never have enough water to fill more than a few inches of the bath. When I passed Duncan's 'office' the other day, the sign, now reading simply ASER UMBER, was hanging quite straight. The old man is back in business.

Autumn 1969

Shampoo and Set   by Phyllis M. Booth

'Closed for extensive alterations' said the notice in our village hairdresser's (Jeanette—Ladies' Hair Styliste), where we had been shampooed and set for twenty years, quietly, pleasantly and, let us admit, without much variation in style. Of course, we knew all about the alterations; Jeanette had been talking of nothing else for months. The village was growing all the time, trade was booming and big things were being planned for her customers. She even hinted that she might be employing more staff. This was rather puzzling, as we never saw anybody but Jeanette on the premises, though the establishment did close for 'staff holidays' during one week in August when she herself went to Bournemouth. So Jeanette locked us out and drew her blinds on the mysterious hammerings and sawings within. That is how two of her clients, shaken out of their routine, came to be venturing into a hairdressing establishment in the nearest town, ready after a hard morning's shopping to relax for an hour or so.

A delightful wave of warm scented air met us as we fumbled our way in through rather odd glass doors. Our feet sank into the pink carpet: why did Mary's sensible brogues look so large and dirty all of a sudden? Two exotic beings with eyelids glinting green and gold removed our hats, coats, scarves, gloves, umbrellas, parcels and shopping bags. 'Just keep your handbags', they said; but Mary's shopping bag is one of those with the purse in an outside pocket, so she chose to remain burdened.

In the salon, arrayed in stiff shocking-pink smocks which did nothing for our ruddy country complexions, we were seated, combed, equipped with magazines and left to survey our surroundings: rows of women everywhere being permed, shampooed, dried, brushed, combed and prinked. It was all very interesting to us after the curtained, cubicled privacy of Jeanette's.

Monsieur himself approached to greet us and take stock. His comments as he tripped over Mary's shopping bag were only just audible. She glanced suspiciously at his pointed Italian-style shoes while he gave her a long appraising stare. The crisis passed; he snapped his fingers once, twice, and hissed loudly across the salon, 'Two mesdames for washing'. A little later, when we had been across to the line of wash-bowls and were back in his hands, he did his best for us, with much posturing and gesturing which were a joy to watch. Then over to the line of driers, with Mary still humping her shopping and murmuring that when she was a child at parties they did it to music.

Half an hour later I was looking frantically at my watch and trying to catch Monsieur's eye. Eventually a satellite pronounced us dry and led us, still on the conveyor belt, back to the centre of the salon. Monsieur himself advanced, brush in hand, ready for the supreme final touch; but Mary had had enough: 'No, I won't have it combed out tonight'. There was a horrified silence, an expressive Gallic shrug, and we prepared to depart. Hastily, as we paid at the desk, we calculated ten per cent of the bills and, with an embarrassed 'Please would you do that for us' to the green eyelids, withdrew.

Jeanette is open again now, and Mary and I have been to inspect the extensive alterations. Instead of the single cubicle which we occupied in turn all those years, there are now two private, curtained, self-contained fastnesses, each fitted with its coat-hooks, parcel-rack, mirror, wash-bowel, hair-drier – everything. One enters with the delightful feeling of *j'y suis, j'y reste*. The staff has been augmented by a younger edition of Jeanette – some distant relative who bears an uncanny resemblance to her as she was when she first came to us. Otherwise things are unchanged. The marmalade cat, known to the neighbour's gardener as that damyeller cat, still sits haughtily at the door and demands to be let in or out according to which side he is on. We continue to pay Jeanette her modest charge and supplement it now and then with a dozen eggs or a few special flowers from the garden, and with something more substantial at Christmas. No more extensive alterations are planned, and we are settled again contentedly in our comfortable rut.

Summer 1961

The Benefits of Barbers by J. J. Maling

We had several choices open to us when we wanted a haircut in Diss, the small market town in Norfolk where I lived about 1930.

There was Mr Studd, who had a shop at the top end of Denmark Street and smoked Goldflakes. In those days they had splendid cigarette cards called Do-You-Knows, and a man with the reputation of being a potential supplier could hardly cross the street without being accosted by would-be beneficiaries. So usually I spent my threepence (it was half-price for boys) with him.

Dan Jones was halfway up Pump Hill. He was one of those modern ambitious business men; he first introduced Diss to electric clippers, not to mention hair-dryers and permanent waving, for he also catered for the ladies. As his name suggested Dan was a foreigner from Wales, and, almost inevitably, a tenor. He called himself a professional and demanded a guinea to sing at a local concert. However, he made no charge for singing at his work, and it was a nicely balanced issue as to whether a faintly possible Do-You-Know at Studd's was the equal of the absolute certainty of 'Every valley shall be exalted' at Dan's place.

At the bottom of the hill was a newcomer, Eric Hall. Formerly he had been Dan Jones's apprentice, and his appearance independently at such short range displeased his old employer, who was inclined to drop into Welsh when the matter was mentioned.

But in many ways, the real character among the Diss barbers was Mr Saunders. He alone, disregarding the over-genteel 'hairdresser', called himself a barber. He only charged threepence when others demanded a full sixpence, and twopence for boys. I think most of his regular customers were farm workers, and Mr Saunders too was dressed for the land. I never saw him without his shiny brown leather leggings, but higher up he was rather less smart. His collarless, tieless shirt was fastened with a gleaming brass stud. He was a big man, heavily moustached, with a curly pipe permanently clenched in his teeth. Inside the shop there shone a dim religious light by courtesy of the Diss Gas Company; a flickering naked light above the chair. The local gas works provided a particularly smelly product, but in Mr Saunders's shop the flavour of this was modified by the scent of ripe, sometimes over-ripe apples. Other barbers might sell razor blades and nail files and Anzora Viola, but Mr Saunders only sold apples; he had a bit of land out Fersfield way.

You might have wondered how he could make a living out of threepenny haircuts and apples, but he had a few sidelines. It was one of these that brought me into contact with him.

My father, also a man of many sidelines, was branch secretary of a friendly society called the Foresters, which entitled him to go on the Armistice Day church parade in a green sash. Mr Saunders was also an official of the branch. They called him if I remember rightly, the senior woodward, and it was his job to pay out cash benefits to sick members. Often I had to take him messages, account books or money, and he always gave my mission priority. He would leave the man in the chair with lather all over his face (barbers did not mind doing shaves then; most of them seem to belong to an Anti-Shaving Society now), lead me into his sittingroom next to the shop, and slowly and deliberately do his sums on a scrap of paper before handing me a message to take back. I do not recall that the customer, gently simmering under the gas, ever protested. He would have recognised, no doubt, that big business took precedence over twopenny shaves.

Not that Mr Saunders was some kind of angel of mercy. He thought that all sick members were parasites and scroungers, and every shilling he reluctantly handed over gave him personal pain.

'Ah!' he'd say. 'Do you wait till Yarmouth Day' (that was our town's annual seaside excursion, on which everyone went) 'and all those bedridden chaps'll soon get better, you mark my words. Ah! and be back with a new doctor's certificate the day arter, I shouldn't wonder.'

Autumn 1974

Putting it in Print   by David Hill

In the 500 years since Caxton set up his press at Westminster the printer has become as much a part of the local scene and almost as widespread as smith and farrier. Certainly, even with the decline of small units, no community of market town size or larger can be without its friendly neighbourhood printer.

The pleasures of being a small town jobbing printer are many. One of the first is the amazing variety of orders which pass through one's hands. These vary in size from the smallest of self-adhesive labels, by way of hunt ball invitations and disposal sale catalogues, to double crown posters advertising the letting of marsh grazing. In quantity they range from singles to perhaps half a million and in content from the ridiculous to the sublime.

My advice on how to get the best from your printer is to make a friend of him and to consult with him at an early stage when you have any sort of printing in mind. I must confess that some such consultations have left me feeling that I ought to have taken a form of Hippocratic oath as amended for printers. Others have made me feel like the letterwriter in an Indian village: I have often been left with such instructions as 'Well, you know what to put, I'll leave it to you'. Experience of such clients has taught me to insist on submitting proofs even when the need for such action has been airily waved aside.

It also becomes a fruit of experience to be able to judge when to comment on copy submitted for printing and when to keep quiet. But even the well-tried saying 'When in doubt follow customer's copy' will not always absolve one from censure. 'You ought to have known' is flung out and somehow you feel guilty.

I was once foolish enough to comment about the value of prizes to be printed on some draw tickets in aid of a village church restoration fund. It was evident to me that even the sale of every ticket could not come near to the cost of 'One pig, one bottle of whisky, one box of chocolates and many other fine prizes'.

'Ah,' I was told, 'it's a very small pig'. So I shut up, bought some of the tickets, but sadly failed to win the very small pig.

I also came off second best from an encounter when delivering some funeral service sheets. The little parish church was remote and I was none too sure of my bearings. As I went up the path I met a man with a spade on his shoulder. 'Excuse me, is this St. Mary's church?' 'Ha!', he replied, 'if it ain't I've dug a hole in the wrong place.'

Content of orders, I have said, varies between the ridiculous and the sublime. In the first classification I include many political and campaign leaflets which I am sure will have profited no one but the printer. At the other end of the scale there are full colour illustrated works for estate agents and art galleries: finished products on which one is proud to place a discreet imprint.

Particularly pleasing in this field of work is being brought in at an early stage to help design, plan and finally produce the product, for a jobbing printer is expected to include all such services within a single scale of charges.

Our parish magazine is a joint affair covering about thirty-two churches. The bound volumes form a fascinating social history of the area. We were delighted, as the current printer of the magazine, to help in staging its centenary exhibition last year. Less happy has been my position on the management committee, where so many of our ideas for enlivening the publication are frustrated by the rising costs which I have to justify. The other committee members must often regard me as truly a 'printer's devil'.

Much of one's work is of an ephemeral nature. A great deal of it I know is destined for the waste paper basket, but nevertheless I find in printing a strong element of that old thing known as job satisfaction. A great part of this satisfaction comes from the comfortable feeling of being a useful and well-integrated member of a largely rural community, from the fact that one comes to know so many people and so become even in a small measure involved in their lives.

Such involvement is never more evident than in the choice of wedding stationery, and it is often an event of potential humour. My own daughter's wedding invitation was described by a knowledgeable friend as 'a typographical tour de force', but most of my customers are more conservative in their requirements. I treasure the remark made by one mother-of-the-bride who complained that the hymn which she had chosen looked 'too long and narrow'.

The all-important trivia of human affairs get set in type. Birth announcement cards, party invitations, wedding service sheets, change of address cards and ultimately the funeral order of service. We offer a service from cradle to grave, with Times Roman, Palace Script, Univers, Windsor, Baskerville and hundreds of other typefaces from which to choose. The choice is far wider than Caxton ever knew, and there is always an endless flow of words to print.

Spring 1977

Watchmaker   by Leonard Clark

Last of his line, the watchmaker is dead,
His shop in the village street will soon close,
Another, of this generation, will be opened instead,
'Boutique' or 'Bookmaker', who knows?

Passing his window I used to see him there,
Head bowed over bench, all hours of the day,
Squatting uncomfortably on edge of old chair,
Jeweller's glass in eye, working away.

Peering at dusty pivots until the light went,
With tiny tweezers lifted out cylinder and wheel,
Fingers tense, forehead furrowed with intent,
Dropped oil on each centimetre of steel.

Cigarette dangling, he cursed the small enginry,
Muttered because an escapement would not come right,
Then, to set pinions to their correct degree,
Put on his spectacles, switched on the light.

Strange, though, he was never on time himself,
Uncertain when jobs were ready, would nervously grope
Among his clutter of parts lying on littered shelf;
You left your watch with him in faith and hope.

Would say 'It will be ready, sir, early next week',
Dismissing you gently, disarm with broad smiles,
Knowing you belonged to the company of the meek,
Went back to fiddling with faces and dials.

His hour now struck, he travels out of time,
His seventy years a hairspring, his clock unwound,
His last watch kept, he hears another chime
Where no chronology is ever found.

Autumn 1976

Lamp-lighter Sam   by Marjorie Bell

It was on a storm-wracked afternoon thirty years ago that I first saw Sam. He shuffled towards me enveloped in a monstrous overcoat which reached to his ankles, a can of paraffin suspended from one hand and in the other a short ladder.

'A wretched day', I greeted him.

'Kn-known f-far worse', he stuttered in reply.

Even then I had thought oil street-lamps as obsolete as the dodo, and I stopped to watch him mount the ladder, fill a lamp, polish the glass and trim the wick. A gusty wind blew out his taper many times, but he persisted with unruffled patience till the light burned brightly; then he shouldered his burdens afresh and went on to the next lamp. The landlord of the Kentish inn where I was staying told me that for thirty years at least Sam had lit the lamps in the great straggling village, refusing all offers of help. He made the long round on foot; then at ten o'clock, punctual to the minute, he started off again to put them out one by one.

Next morning I asked the landlord if it was possible to get my watch repaired in the village. 'Oh, yes,' he said, 'take it to old Sam. He'll soon get it going for you. Everyone here'll tell you that the posh jewellers in towns can't compare with him for workmanship'. I found Sam's cottage at the end of a narrow rutted lane; it was a solitary place, but the brick doorstep was freshly 'redded' and the lace curtains at the windows were immaculate. 'Yes?' he demanded truculently in response to my knock. I handed him my watch and asked if it could be repaired. He peered at it and shook it: 'Not a very l-long job, but I c-can't do it today. G-got a f-funeral on. Let you have it t-tomorrow'. That afternoon I chanced to pass the churchyard and there was Sam the sexton standing motionless by the graveside, a serene expression on his face and that absurd overcoat flapping round him.

But it was not till one frosty evening when the heavens were a mass of stars that I discovered the real Sam. He was in the middle of the deserted street and had with him, supported by three sprawling wooden legs, an ancient and cumbersome telescope. He was no longer the simple countryman but a keen scientist whose astronomical knowledge was enormous. From what source he had gained it I do not know. I had seen no array of books when I visited his cottage, yet his familiarity with the names and characteristics of the stars would have put many a student to shame. He talked fluently, with no trace of a stammer, overjoyed at finding someone interested in his hobby, for apparently his star-gazing was a local joke. All too soon he pulled a big watch from his pocket and gave a sigh. Then he turned up the collar of that atrocious overcoat and laid a hand on the telescope. 'T-time to p-put out the l-lamps', he said.

Spring 1957

For Services Rendered   by Joan Tate

Twice daily for six years I had had to drive along nine miles of winding, narrow, hilly country road, between high hedges and steep banks, to a remote village near the Welsh border. I had watched the seasons change and enjoyed the lovely countryside, and every morning I had exchanged salutes with the roadman, who was always there before me. Although I had never spoken to him, I felt he was an old friend. The road was trim, the bridge railing was painted, the banks were kept cut back; the great harvest of cow-parsley was mown down with a sickle just before it leant through the windows on both sides of the car. In winter the treacherous corners and hills were gritted. So, in a burst of energy after a difficult day's driving, I sat down and wrote to the county surveyor to convey my thanks. The polite and formal reply from the office was eventually followed by a letter from the roadman himself. 'Dear Madam,' it ran, 'I have received a copy of your letter from Our County Surveyor which I am pleased to know you are pleased how we try to do our Best for you all and I know Our Surveyors are Grateful to you has they do get so many Unthankfull letters from the Public and I know you will be sorry to know I will be retiring from Road work after Whitsun in June has my wife will be 80 in April and I now feel that it will be my duty to be at home and look after her she is not very strong. I have been working on the Roads over 40 years and I think you may see a Record of my life in the papers and my native home is London. Thanking you for my good report on my

Most villages once had their own lengthman, or roadman, who cut the verges, cleared gullies, mended walls and generally kept the community's roadways in good order. One of the few survivors is Mr S. Clarke, seen at Honister Pass in the Lake District. (*William S. Paton*)

work. I shall always keep it in my home'. I am glad I wrote, and I shall certainly keep the roadman's letter. It must be very hard to replace such men.

Winter 1960

The Roadman's Flowers   E. Higgs, Worcestershire

As I travelled about the lanes in our roadman's district I would come across occasional clumps of purple knapweed, blue meadow cranesbill or pink rest-harrow that had been spared the scythe and were growing strongly among the well-cut grasses. Puzzled, I stopped one day to chat with him over his garden hedge on the outskirts of the village. We spoke of the trim stone cottage, the weather and the rooks. Yes, he told me, he enjoyed watching the creatures about him as he worked; and he liked flowers. Here he must have noticed my glance at the garden which, though immaculately tidy, contained not a single bloom. 'No,' he went on, 'not in the garden. 'Er always did the flowers there. So I leaves meself bunches by the roadside'.

Autumn 1962

The Art of Rat-Catching   by Andrew Soutar

Old Spike is our rat-catcher. He has a character of his own. He reads the newspapers, takes an interest in politics, formulates opinions about public figures and, with sardonic humour, blends these opinions with his trade. Thus, he will address a particularly vicious old dog rat by the name of some politician for whom he has no particular liking, and, as he cracks him on the head, he will observe that: ' 'Twould gi'e me no pain to gi'e t'other feller a sock aside th' heid like that.' He is moved to admiration of the small and energetic rat that will take unusual risks in a chicken-run when searching for food. He calls him the little Chancellor. ' 'E don't care who got the food; 'e will get it! ' Only once did I find Old Spike communicative about the tricks of his trade. The only trap that seemed serviceable to me was the oblong wire cage with the baited hook and the spring door. The other form of trap, wire-domed and fitted with a tin plate that drops like a hangman's trapdoor when the rat sets foot on it, always appeared to me to be slightly beneath the intelligence of the average rat. But, Old Spike said: 'That's the best trap, but you got to bait 'im, not with cheese or 'erring, but with a rat itself. Catch one in the other trap and pop 'im into this one. Now, feed 'im, gi'e 'im milk, a bit o' meat and see what 'appens', Twenty-five rats in the one trap were the result, for, as Old Spike explained, a rat on the outside, seeing a friend of his within, sleek and well supplied with food, wouldn't rest until he had got in alongside him. One of the baits that Old Spike used on occasion was a drop of aniseed oil.

Never ask a professional rat-catcher what he does with his catch. I have met Old Spike with a sack half full of live rats, but he wouldn't tell me how or where he'd destroy them. He would dive a hand into the sackful of squirming rodents and bring one out for my inspection. He never expected to be bitten, he said, until he was fool enough to put his hand into the sack when there was only one rat left.

I think Old Spike is honest, for he has a fine sense of justice. The farmers employ him to make periodical visits to their barns and stacks, paying him a fixed sum to keep their farms clear. But they have told me of one farmer who thought twice before he parted with a penny. He met Old Spike in the market place, one day, and said to him: 'I'm going to pay you for the last quarter, Spike, but I shan't want you again. I'm satisfied there are no rats left.' Old Spike thanked him courteously, pocketed the money and went his way. Within a week the farmer was complaining that he had never known so many rats about his place. Someone said to him: 'You'd better get Old Spike to come up again.' 'I suppose I must,' said the farmer, 'but I haven't seen him around this district of late'. But, those who knew Old Spike and suspected his ways, fancied that he must have paid the farmer a visit without being seen, and not empty-handed.

The rat is surrounded by many fallacies. He hasn't much courage. He will die of fright in a trap. He puts up a miserable fight against a good terrier and the ferret regards him with a great deal of contempt. Some say that he is extraordinarily cunning and very shrewd in his guesses at the nature of a trap. It isn't so. Compared with the mole, who will keep away from a trap that has been touched with the hand, he is a stupid, greedy, slow-witted fellow. He strikes terror into the hearts of womenfolk by the awful noise he makes when gnawing the skirting boards. It is as though he were burrowing his way in, determined to get at what might lie on the other side. In truth, he is only sharpening those long teeth of his, because, unless he keeps them down, they grow so long as to interfere with his eating. A terrier, sniffing at the wainscoting on the other side, will frighten him away for a long period. One thing I have noticed is that a cat that becomes a rat-catcher (and I have known one actually to jump into a brook after a vole), is seldom any use for keeping down mice. On the other hand, you may have a terrier that will show as much enthusiasm in the catching of mice as in the shaking of a rat.

In view of the thousands of pounds of damage done every year by the rats in the country and the danger of their spreading disease, every district should be encouraged to keep down rats. The usual method of the authorities is to pay a reward on production of tails. Old Spike says that if he had the paying to do he would much rather see the heads. I don't know exactly what he means by that, but there is something sinister in his eyes.

October 1931

Landgirl Ratcatcher*   J.B., Women's Land Army

Three names are on my list, two of them farms, one a butcher's shop. The shop proves to be small and dark and quite unsuitable for the sale of food. 'Overrun with rats', the butcher tells me. They are coming up from the cellar through a hole they have gnawed in the side of a trap-door. With difficulty I get the door open, and crawl down stone steps thick with years of accumulated dirt and made slippery by the feet of the rats, so that I can hardly get a footing. High up in a wall of the dark little cellar is a tiny window with no glass but with broken wire-netting to keep out leaves and grass. The rats have been coming through the broken netting and slithering down the grimy wall.

Now I lay my first feed, chiefly flour and sugar – some on the sides of the stone steps, some around the walls, some in a corner of the window ledge. I never lay it in the open, for the rat likes to keep under cover on his travels. Then I climb out of the dismal hole and go outside to follow up the tracks of the rats before they enter the cellar. This is not difficult, for there is fresh snow. The house and shop are built on the side of a stream – or is drain not the right word? At the top of the bank I find several large rat-holes, and with my longhandled spoon I put down more rat feed.

My next place is a large farm, to which I am paying my second visit. In the byre with its steamy atmosphere, while the cattle are steadily chewing, I put more feed high up on the wall heads, then go on an inspection of stables, sheds and barns. The rats are coming from what was once a mill. The old water-wheel is still there, and I glance at the gleaming black water far below. I take my torch and descend the ladder, hampered by my bag and spoon. It is pitch dark, while all I can hear is the drip-drip of water. When my eyes get used to the gloom I find I am in a dirty chamber with many traces of rats. I put down several doses of feed and pass through into another and smaller place in which there seems to be no air. My torch is flickering and the next minute the battery fails and I am left in total darkness. I must get out. Making for the ladder, I feel round the walls for the door, but find nothing but the cold damp stones – no door, no opening. I go round several times, feeling carefully with my hands, but there is no door. I have a moment of panic, then common sense and reason come to my aid. I got into this place; there must be a way out. Did I not stoop low at one point? I try feeling the walls again but at a much lower level, and here's the opening and I am breathing fresh clean air and am out in the sparkling snow.

My last visit is to a farm high up near the Roman wall. I have not been here before. The sun is sinking and black snow-clouds are piling up. It is darker, and snow is beginning to fall. At last I come out on the road.

[*The author adds*: Every farm and shop is visited three or more times, generally with a day between each visit. Bait is laid in runs and holes. When I know where rats are running I can put down the poison.]

*As many as 200 of the 850 rat-catchers under the Government scheme are members of the Women's Land Army. It is estimated that every rat on a farm costs the farmer 6s a year, and that the value of food and feeding-stuffs in this country eaten or spoilt by rats amounts to £25,000,000 a year!

Winter 1942

The Knacker   by H.C.

The cow could not last much longer in such a state. It was too late, anyhow – the knacker had been phoned for. An unwholesome, facetious old man, his trade evident from his gory black clothes, he appeared leading a horse and cart. The horse looked as if it had been assembled from parts of all the dead horses that had been through its driver's hands. On the soiled cart one could make out the words, LICENSED HORSE AND CATTLE SLAUGHTER-MAN. The knacker was in a hurry. 'Show her I', he said, 'and the job won't take a jiffy.' He backed his cart to the door of the loose-box in which the beast was panting. Planks were laid to the cart, and a winch was rigged with which to haul her up, a chain being slipped round her neck. The executioner deftly lifted the unresisting head from the ground, and with a smart tap from his much-worn block of wood the job was done. The winch rattled and squeaked, and the half ton or so of cats' meat (one hopes) was dragged into the cart. The head stuck out at the front and lolled down beside a shaft; the knacker climbed up, sat on the corpse's neck, and gave his horse the whip. The head began to swing beside the horse's flank, the tongue hanging out grotesquely.

Summer 1942

The Happy Undertaker　　　　　　by Marian E. Noble

The happiest man I knew was our village undertaker. When not engaged in reverently following the departed to their final resting-place, or kindly consoling their sorrowing relations, he was enjoying life as hilariously as he possibly could. One of his pastimes was to charge round the countryside in his second-best hearse, filled chock-a-block with friends, stopping only to quench their thirst at convenient pubs.

He was known affectionately as Uncle Tommy to all the local children, though he had none of his own. His great love, apart from his blonde and vivacious wife, was animals; when he spoke of them his big brown eyes softened and his pert moustache bristled. His pocket-handkerchief garden, which ran parallel to the photographer's where I worked, was crammed full of creatures – two or three dogs, pigs, cats and dozens of kittens, as well as chickens, ducks and geese chuckling and quacking contentedly. Tommy loved every feather and pair of trusting eyes, and could not bear to part with any of them. Only with the pigs would he reluctantly compromise, realising that Sally the sow, whom he helped through her frequent confinements, could not keep her litters for ever.

One day, having decided to stand for election to the local council, Tommy came round to our studio at the bottom of the garden to have his portrait taken. His top half was immaculate in white shirt and black coat, with just the right sort of tie to gain the voters' confidence: the other half was clad in an old pair of jodhpurs and manure-spattered boots. 'Don't worry about that, me dear', he said, noticing my down-swept glance. 'I only want head and shoulders, and I'm exercising me mare afterwards, so I didn't bother to change.'

The mare was the latest addition to the menagerie. She grazed part of the time in a near-by meadow, but Tommy had built her a stable in his garden next to the pigsty. Over the wall wafted a medley of odours – pig-swill cooking on the old boiler, horse manure and disinfectant – but we never thought of complaining. The photographer and Tommy were the best of friends and enjoyed many a pint as they sat side by side on one of the coffins in Tommy's workroom or the old sea chest which served as our photographic seat.

'That mare of yours is too fat', said my boss. 'Give her a bit more exercise.'

So every day, except when employed in his occasional under-taking or campaigning as the working man's friend in opposition to both Labour and Conservative candidates, Tommy would gallop up and down the street and out to the common. In spite of his efforts the mare lost no weight, until one morning, going down with the hay, Tommy saw to his delight a new-born foal. Evidently the mare had done more than graze during her days in the meadow. This provided another job for the photographer.

Tommy won the election with a resounding majority and was soon chairman of the entertainments committee. The highlight of his year was 'Holidays at Home' week, when the common and manor house were thrown open to the public and decorated for a week of festivity, with a different event each day. Tommy was in his element arranging bunting and ordering marquees. He judged the dogs on Monday, patted the babies' heads on Tuesday, and on Saturday superintended the annual horse show and beauty

queen contest. By this time he was so inebriated with excitement
that he hardly knew whether he was pinning a blue rosette on his
favourite charger or handing a silver cup to the winning Miss
Mortonsfield.

Sad was the day when all his friends read his obituary in the
local paper. They mourned him in his favourite haunts, started
a collection at the Red Lion and sent a deputation to his wife to
offer their condolences. 'Tommy dead?' she gasped. 'He was all
right when I saw him a few minutes ago'; and much to their
amazement she led the party down the garden to where Tommy
was cleaning out his new rabbit-hutch.

No-one ever found out whether that premature announcement
was the work of a practical joker, or even Tommy's own way of
raising a macabre laugh. As far as I know, the happy undertaker
is still living blithely in the village I left long ago.

Spring 1963

All Made By Hand

Country Potter   **by John Manners**

The country potters who were born to the trade have all but
vanished, and there are probably less than half-a-dozen left,
though there is a superfluity of artist-trained potters making a
good living with more sophisticated ware using attractive glazes.

The traditional country potter plied his trade where there was
a good supply of suitable clay, whereas the artist-potter first finds
his premises and then orders his clay to be delivered by the
hundredweight.

A doyen of country potters is Rowland Curtis, in his mid-70s,
of Littlethorpe, near Ripon in Yorkshire, who has been at his
wheel since leaving school about 60 years ago. His products are
mostly large ornamental garden pots that weigh around 20 to
30lb before firing, though there is a steady demand for smaller
ones which most serious gardeners prefer to the plastic type. He
can throw up to 40lb of clay, the size of the pot being limited by
the length of the arm.

Whereas he used to throw a ton of clay a day, he now works
part-time and uses a ton a week; this, which his son digs by
shovel, is used immediately without any weathering. First the
clay is fed into the pugging machine which mixes it up ready for
use. A piece of clay is cut off, weighed and then wedged by
slamming it down on the bench for a minute or two to eliminate
any air bubbles. Mr Curtis next throws the lump of clay on to
his power-driven wheel and works it upwards and outwards, so
that in five minutes the lump emerges as a smooth and beauti-
fully-proportioned pot with a thick lip on top to give it a finish.
His skill makes it all look disarmingly easy.

As an additional embellishment a coil of clay may be put around
the pot and a patterned design added with the fingers, and finally
all pots are stamped with the maker's name. A piece of wire
severs the pot from the wheel, and Mr Curtis picks up his huge

pot in his hands and places it on a drying bench. The drying process is helped by gentle heat, and once a week the production is carefully packed into a large electric kiln for firing.

By a fortunate chance his clay contains some magnesium, which helps to make it the finest horticultural clay there is. Supplies are more or less unlimited even after the 135 years the pottery has been in existence.

Mr Curtis has seen some ups and downs in his time. In the 1920s country potters were kept busy making bread crocks, bowls for setting milk and cooling pots for cream, all of which were glazed. In addition they all made flower pots which can be turned out at an incredible speed. The trade was killed by plastic pots, soil and peat blocks, and the potters rapidly went out of business. Mr Curtis was forced to give up for two years and keep poultry in his pottery sheds, but his one-man business is now thriving. He sells direct, never advertises and cannot cope with the demand, knowing of no competitor within hundreds of miles.

He has occasionally taught his craft in the past but cannot do so now as he has no diploma. Thus the man with the most experience of throwing pottery in the country is prevented from passing on his skill and knowledge to future generations.

He gets some amusement from the forms he is regularly sent to fill in from the government department responsible for mines,

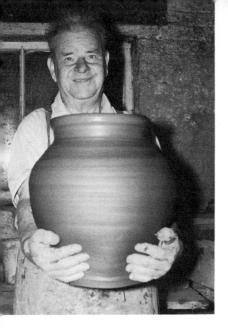

Rowland Curtis, now in his 70s, still makes garden pots by hand at Littlethorpe in York-shire. Here he raises a 20lb giant and carries its satisfying bulk to the kiln (*John Manners*)

which call for hundreds of answers. He is able to fill in but one of the questions, against which he writes '00 shovel'. This is the shovel with which the clay is dug and he is sure the recipient of the answer is not sufficiently educated to understand the answer.

His prowess has not brought him any great riches, though he is able to live comfortably. In his mid-70s he is thankful to have health and strength which are more valuable than money.

Spring 1976

Thinking about Elm   by Thomas Hudson

Elm is a timber that I do not use much these days. True I made a seat for a rocking chair recently and I do like to put an elm top on a coffee table, but, as I say, it is regrettably not found in my workshop as much as it used to be.

It was turning some wet elm the other day for fruit bowls that made me think about it, because that in itself is a rare occurrence. I had cut up some elm from a tree that had come down during a gale a couple of years ago and after tussling with an axe, beetle and wedges, I at last got it on to the lathe. Of course one pur-chases suitable dry elm today in ready squared pieces which makes things a little easier but I felt that this time such an exercise as taking it from the tree would be spiritually rewarding

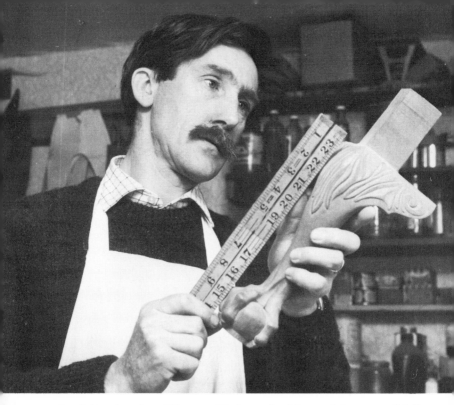

Specialist in elm, Thomas Hudson, in his workshop at Odell, Bedfordshire. (*Northampton Chronicle and Echo*)

although I was aware that if I counted my time it would be a dead loss.

If you have never seen wet elm being turned on a lathe you have missed one of the simple pleasures in life. With a good sharp tool the wood streams off amidst the pungent flying sap. Ever-changing patterns grow and diminish before you as the contours of grain spin against the tool in your hand. Before long you are standing ankle deep in the delicately soft product of nature. At the end of it all you are left with a very thick bowl shape which should be left for some months to dry out before cutting to its final form. By removing the waste before drying, the seasoning time is considerably reduced and also a more stable bowl is obtained at the finish.

Of course, years ago, elm was much in demand in country workshops for such things as chair seats, wheelbarrows, coffins, tools and farm equipment as well as for numerous articles for everyday village life. It is a remarkable timber for so many purposes. Some parts of it are impossible to split and, as it is durable in water, village pumps were always of elm and water pipes were made from it too, before the use of metal ones.

Making such pipes was indeed a task for the craftsman, considering that he drilled these out by hand with a long auger through the elm bough while it was still 'green'. He drilled from both ends and met in the middle. Considerable strength was necessary to turn such an auger as it was often ten foot long and up to eight inches across.

Its resistance to splitting was the reason for wheel hubs or 'naves' to be always of elm. The fact that much of it was drilled out for spokes and axle did not weaken a good hub. Imagine the stress on a farm cart wheel, swaying under its heavy load, clattering over cobbles and rutted roads, sometimes swimming in mud. Round and round went the wooden wheel, held together and to the cart through all the seasons and changes of weather by the elm hub. Such elm was carefully selected by men who had learned their trade from boyhood, and pride in a fine article was felt through the whole workshop. Unless such a wheel lasted indefinitely the farmer or carter would want an explanation from the wheelwright!

Well now, you can see why I use little elm today in my country workshop, where the call is for handmade furniture and repairs, but still when I look at the great elms standing not far from my house, I think of the incredible work that has been done with it, not just in country workshops, but round the coasts where piers have stood on it, capstans and breakwaters have been made from it, and the keels of great ships.

If you get the chance to look at a fruit bowl or other article made from this timber, remember with me, as you regard the tough interlocked beauty of its grain structure lying so quietly, how it has insisted through the ages that only an experienced man could harness and make full use of its fine qualities.

Autumn 1971

A Yorkshire Woodcarver   by G. Bernard Wood

When Thomas Whittaker arrived in Littlebeck soon after the 1939–45 war he had been given only two years to live; but he has outlasted his doctors and given new life to this Yorkshire village. The small community has expanded in size and self-esteem, and it now has a first-rate village hall built by local volunteers. Whittaker initiated the project and himself undertook most of the heavy woodwork for it. One of his first tasks was to fit up the former Bay Horse Inn as his home. He calls it St Hilda, after the famous Abbess of Whitby Abbey, whence monks used to bring pannier-laden beasts this way. It was the monks' hospitium chapel in early days, and the lounge was then the stable. His workshop, built with his own hands, stands high above the beck, facing the house on the other side.

He plainly regards it as part of his mission to recapture the monastic heritage of the place and give it a new context. An example is the pair of carvings on the entrance gates to the old mill, which he helped to restore and convert into a private house: one shows Whitby Abbey as it stands today, the other a thurible and altar candles. They symbolise an old custom whereby the Abbot of Whitby let the grazing rights hereabouts to the Prior of Bridlington for an annual payment, on St Hilda's Day, of a pound of incense and a pound of wax for use in the abbey.

Many of Whittaker's ancestors were woodcarvers in Lancashire, where he was born. Of one he was given a strange reminder when a monk from the Collegio de Inglesis at Valladolla, Spain, visited Littlebeck to order a statue of the Virgin Mary for his monastery. When it was finished the craftsman had to slash the Virgin's cheeks and cut off her nose, as it was to be an exact replica of one which Drake's men had mutilated with their cutlasses at Cadiz. Whittaker had been chosen to carve this statue because, unknown to him, one of his ancestors, a Lancashire woodcarver of the same name, took monastic vows at the Collegio de Inglesis; he was later martyred for his faith at Lancaster in 1646.

Thomas Whittaker is now the only member of the family working on traditional lines. He studied anatomy and sculpture at an art school, and later travelled round to gain experience in

Thomas Whittaker, of Littlebeck, Yorkshire, carves a lion's head on a faldstool he is making. (*G. Bernard Wood*)

woodcarving; he spent three months with Bob Thompson, the famous ecclesiastical craftsman, at Kilburn, near York. He designs all his own work, being a great admirer of the Germanic school. In his workshop, where he is assisted by two men and a youth, there is always something being made in a style that recalls the medieval carvers who worked in our abbeys and cathedrals. The credences of pre-Reformation times offer good scope for first-rate carving. One made here has a handle in the form of a clenched hand to indicate that, in its original use as a receptacle for the Holy Sacrament, only the priest had access.

Not all the emphasis is on the past. Among the figure carvings I have seen, King Alfred and Guthrum the Dane are at one end of the time scale and Bernard Shaw at the other. But most of Whittaker's work represents a culture that reached its zenith in the Ripon school of woodcarvers (fifteenth and sixteenth centuries) and similar schools elsewhere. When he makes a gate of overlapping planks, or fashions a refectory tabletop from two tapering boards that follow the shape of the tree, he is not only using old skills but also passing on their benefits to a new age.

All his constructional tools are traditional: the adze, draw-knife and wood chisel. A plane rarely touches his work. He uses circular and band saws to cut up heavy timber, for economy and to give him more time for the other work, which is all done by hand. It takes a clever craftsman to use the adze, which has a curved blade fixed at right angles to the end of a long shaft. Swung with the action of a pick, it peels the surface of the wood, leaving slight undulations that bring out the full beauty of the grain. Other craftsmen make his wrought-iron fittings, and prepare the hide for chair seats. This hide, he says, must last as long as the chair; and that means three or four centuries, for he intends his work to survive at least as long as the misericords, carved newels and leather-covered benches of Tudor times.

When I last saw him he was completing for his workshop entrance a signboard showing many gnomes busily at work among the trees – felling, sawing, carving and so on. A tiny gnome, often contained within a small Gothic arch, is the symbol he carves on every piece of work. It is derived from a Nordic legend which relates that, when an acorn sprouts, there is born a gnome which grows up with the tree, caring for it through every vicissitude. As Whittaker works exclusively in English oak, the gnome is an apt little guardian for the faldstools, altar rails, pulpits, lecterns and other pieces of furniture which now go from Littlebeck to many parts of the world.

Summer 1959

Craft with Progress   by Norah Marshall

It is difficult to think of Edward Gardiner of Priors Marston as seventy-four. Tall and thin, he has the animation of a young man and, under his unruly mop of white hair, a forward-looking mind. As a chairmaker he still keeps up the traditional country craft handed down to him from Philip Clissett through Ernest Gimson, but at the same time he strives continually after new and labour-saving devices, so that the same high-quality article may be made more easily. He will work for years to perfect a gadget, such as that which holds the back legs of a chair at just the right angles for making the holes to take the staves, slats and arms. This is fixed to the lathe which he has been using for nearly half a century; originally worked by water, then by gas-engine, it is now powered by an up-to-date electric motor. The harnessing of past and present is seen also when the back legs, cut and turned in the green, are boiled in an electric copper, bent in an ancient-looking press and then stacked in a shed which has been converted into a thermostatically controlled drying-house.

In another workshop I found Gardiner's assistant, Victor Neal, weaving seats with rushes harvested locally from the Leam and Avon, while Victor's son Neville worked on the slats for chair-backs at an incredibly old 'horse'. This was once Gimson's – nothing modern would serve better – but again that active mind which never hesitates to graft an improvement on to the old-but-sound had been at work and a piece of motor-tyre had been added to give a better grip. Looking ahead to the day when he must retire, Gardiner has encouraged the Neals to fit up a little workshop in their own village of Stockton, and he passes over to them some of his orders to complete in their spare time. I arrived when he was finishing 'a grand saw-up'. Ash, oak and yew lay all around ready for sorting, wood with a natural curve being set aside for rockers and arms. Nothing is wasted: even the sawdust is burnt to heat the shop.

Gardiner's story begins about 1894, when his father had a farm in the Gloucestershire hamlet of Pinbury, near Cirencester; the only neighbours were the carter, shepherd and coalman. Those were hard times for farmers, and after a succession of bad seasons the young Edward decided to help his grandfather who owned a sawmill at near-by Sapperton. Meanwhile the Elizabethan manor house on the hill above Pinbury, once the home of Sir Robert Atkyns, the Gloucestershire historian, had been rented by 'young college gentlemen' and there were rumours of 'strange goin's on'. It seemed that they made fine furniture and silver and iron work, and that they did the queerest things: why, they had made for a church a great oak cross, later to be covered in metal, and had actually carried it down the valley and laid it in the bed of the stream.

The newcomers were Ernest Gimson, who made himself a

Chairmaker Neville Neal works at Gimson's 'horse', while his father plaits a seat. (*John Saunders*)

cottage from an old farm building behind the house, and Ernest and Sidney Barnsley. They were disciples of William Morris, whose aim was to preserve and develop the traditional design and craftsmanship that were in danger of being lost in the machine age. They had trained as architects but set themselves to learn and practise allied crafts, believing with Morris that nothing should be done in their workshops which they could not do themselves. It was when they went to order wood from the Sapperton sawmill that Edward Gardiner met them and became fascinated by the beauty of the things they made.

In 1903 the three friends moved to Sapperton, where they rented Daneway, a large and beautiful medieval house, for workshops and showrooms; and Gimson built for himself in the village the thatched stone cottage where he lived for the rest of his life. At almost the same time Edward Gardiner's grandfather died, and he went with his father to live in the old mill at Sapperton. Meanwhile, in the village of Bosbury in Herefordshire, Gimson had found an old man named Philip Clissett who continued to make chairs in the traditional way, turning the parts on a simple pole-lathe and seating the chairs with rushes. Here he spent some time learning the craft.

On his return to Sapperton, Gimson asked to be allowed to set up his lathe at the Gardiners' mill and work it by water-power. 'You can bring the lathe and let young Edward turn the parts for you; he could do with more work' was the reply. At first Edward did not do very well: he was making only parts, without understanding the uses to which they would be put. Then Gimson, who was busy on a dining-table, showed him the design for the matching chairs and let him make a complete one. Suddenly everything fell into place in his mind. When Gimson saw the chair finished except for the rush seat, he declared: 'You have the gift; you must go on with it'. So they entered into a gentlemen's agreement by which Gimson obtained orders and designed the chairs, which were made by Gardiner, the profits being shared. The first chairs Gardiner took on horseback to an old man at Nailsworth who seated them for 2s 9d apiece; but it was a long journey over the hills into the next valley and he decided to seat the next ones himself. When his first consignment of rushes, which came from salt water, proved unsatisfactory he rode to Cricklade to fetch some from the Thames, and these served well.

Thus Gardiner combined chairmaking with sawmilling until 1913, when he moved to Cubbington, near Leamington, in search of flatter country and greater opportunities; but just as he was settling down, war came and chairmaking was forgotten. When, in 1919, Sidney Barnsley wrote asking him to make, for the war-memorial library at Bedales School, sixty chairs which Gimson had designed just before his death the same year, Gardiner pleaded that he was too busy with sawmilling; his benches and some of his tools were gone, and his patterns and lathe packed away. Back came the answer: 'If you will not, there is no-one else who can make them as he would have wished'. So out came the tools, a new bench was set up and the chairs began to take shape. From that order came many more, from the Dean and Chapter of Coventry Cathedral, from the London County Council and from individuals, and when he moved to Priors Marston, near Rugby, in 1928, chairmaking was his full-time occupation.

Again war brought discouragement, and when the rural industries organiser for Warwickshire found him six years ago he was almost on the point of giving up because of shortages, permits, purchase tax and soaring prices. Help from the machinery and costing officers of the Rural Industries Bureau and opportunities to demonstrate his craft on the rural community council's stands at shows kept him going.

Gimson's furniture was once described as 'useful and right, perfectly shaped and finished, and good enough (but not too good) for ordinary use'. It is an apt description of the chairs of Edward Gardiner.

Spring 1956

Farm Waggon   by M. A. B. Jones

Discarded, lying derelict
Year-long in the High Acre, it lost caste.
Active young men riding tractors
Trailing latest attachments
Beetled importantly past.

Restored it shines centrepiece
In a farm museum. Oak bodywork,
The floor elm-lined, speaks of his antique skill,
The wheelwright's practised eye, his certain hand.

Choosing tough hedgewood, weathered ash,
He used the adze to carve the inner curve
Of felloes, cut for hubs – a single mortice-stroke
Sufficed – wych elm well-twisted from the hard
Trunk growth. The high wide wheels strake-tyred,
Metal handforged. Spokes cleft, not sawn.
Shafts clearly fashioned for the horse.

Raves planed, the heavy timbers shaved
To lighten weight, the whole lightpainted
Rode well in the corn. And the craftsman's son,
Seeing the coloured wheels submissive turn,
A man at last, willing at once to learn.

Autumn 1975

More than Wheels by Jocelyn Bailey

Ours is an old village wheelwright's business, and the workshop is much in its original condition, complete with cobwebbed windows, earthen floor, the scent of fresh wood shavings and shadowy glimpses of many old tools placed in dusty rows, silent sentinels of an age we can never fully visualize.

My husband was taught the craft by his father, who in turn was apprenticed to my husband's maternal grandfather, though just how long it goes back in the family we do not know.

He has gradually explained the names and uses of some of the tools peculiar to the trade. My favourite is 'Samson', probably 200 years old, made of iron and used in early wheelmaking to grip the finished wooden wheel together in order to be able to nail on the last iron 'strake', which is one of a series of strips of iron nailed around to form a tyre – a method used before the black-smith's method of shrinking a complete band or iron on to the wheel.

A wheelwright works with a complete absence of drawings, diagrams or textbooks. He just seems to take up bits of wood and without any great fuss soon has recognisable parts which he fits together to form a finished article like a perfect poem or piece of music. This instinctive way of working seems to be the essence of the old crafts that were handed from one generation to the next, and extended to a natural feel for the right pieces and varieties of wood to choose for certain work.

One side of the village wheelwright's work was an under-taking business. In our case this was discontinued during the 1939–45 war when my husband was in the Forces. But I am still regaled (usually at mealtimes) with various stories of this side of the business. The wheelwright would make the coffins himself, and usually had known the dead person quite well. Thus it was an emotional involvement, and probably accounted for the noisy 'jokes' which I suppose served to relieve the tension of such a job. My mother-in-law dealt with the arrangement of the coffin linings; I am not too sorry that this side of the business no longer exists. February was the peak month in this line, and my husband tells me his mother would say of the deceased, so-and-so 'didn't manage to get up February hill'.

The names of the main parts of an old wheel are few and simple; the nave (hub), the spokes, the felloes (sections forming the perimeter) and the tyre. The special tools too have quaint names. A 'buzz' is used for cutting the mortices in the nave. The 'adze' scoops out the concave side of the felloe.

Nowadays there is not much full-scale wheelwright's work to be done, but there is a steady call for repairs to old wheels and vehicles for collections. Most of our work now is for general carpentry, farm and house repairs, painting and decorating and other quite varied and often unexpected jobs – a cowl made for an old oast-house or a part made for the restoration of an old mill. Field gates are still in demand and we still feel needed in the shrinking rural setting.

Spring 1974

Pit sawing (*Marcus Beaver*)

Wheelwrights at work (*Marcus Beaver*)

Wheelwright   by Clive Sansom

When Frank was young and huge as a Clydesdale,
He chose the timber for this cart,
Measured the wood and seasoned it,
Then shaped each interlocking part.

Those two great wheels to take the load-weight,
And every axle, shaft and spoke:
Elm for the massive planks and stocks,
The starring wheel-spokes turned from oak.

He built it well. For forty years
His waggon carried muck to spread,
Swung with its towering load of hay
And hauled the harvest to the shed. . .

Then tractors shouldered it aside,
Hub-deep in nettle, vetch and gorse,
It shares this corner of the farm
With horse-plough and a pensioned horse.

And here it stands, all life behind,
Drag-shoe and drip-chain long since gone.
Some spokes are gaps, like missing teeth,
The floor-planks worn by rain and sun,

While Frank, forgotten in his ward,
With dwindled frame and silent tongue,
Remembers in dim happiness
When wheelwright, wheels and world were young.

Spring 1976

Cut and Shut   by David Jeffery, Surrey

To Tom the farrier I mentioned a friend who was looking for a
half-timbered cottage; he had found two or three, but both he and
his wife were tall and had banged their heads several times on the
low door-lintels. 'P'raps 'e could do with a cut and shut', grinned
Tom; and I asked him what he meant. In days gone by, when the
wooden wheels of farm carts shrank in a hot summer, the rims
came off. They were then taken to a wheelwright, who cut the
rims, removed a small portion and spliced, reforged and refitted
them.

Winter 1967

A Master of his Craft   by Sir W. Beach Thomas

For about 200 years the family of the village blacksmith has been
exercising its craft in the same village in the Home Counties, and
to-day's representative has the artist's or craftsman's tempera-
ment and philosophy as strongly, in his strong way, as anyone
in Chelsea. He says of his work, 'I know it is good because I am
pleased with it myself'. He has his limitations as well as his
virtues. For example, he has deserted horses as surely as horses
have deserted him. Shoeing them entailed a nervous exhaustion
which kept him awake at nights. Happily the absence of his
standard job does not involve any loss of work. There has grown
up a demand for curves and crisps at least as seductive in outline
as any horse's shoe, though that should be regarded as not less
truly a work of art than any ornamental gate or cresset. The
blacksmith, in his rough and simple forge, has requests for iron

work from places – to mention particular orders – as far apart
as Cairo and Aberdeen. He manufactures – a good word that has
acquired a mendacious meaning – iron gates, cresset lamps,
brackets, coal scuttles, door knockers, hinges, plates, locks, signs,
vanes, and tools of all sorts. No hammered iron work comes amiss.
The one thing that you may not suggest is that he should use
the file. If he sees a bit of work where the file has been called in to
correct the hammer, he grows furious as any painter whose rival
has scraped high lights with a pen-knife. The file means bad
art, and that is the sin of sins. When he has a big bit of work on
hand (with curves perhaps as difficult to get right as any that
made Aubrey Beardsley's fame) he falls on with fury, scorning
sleep, leisure or any more lucrative job. He would, if need
were, like Benvenuto Cellini, burn his household furniture to
keep the fire hot. And the work, thanks to hereditary knowledge
and craftsman's ideal, is always sterling. He is content as a rule
to borrow his patterns though he is a born designer. But the little
adaptations often amount to a design in themselves, and now and
then he breaks out in stark originality. When the old village fire
engine, whose activities he had directed, was scrapped, his affec-
tions were so moved that he bought the copper boiler, a hand
beaten one at least a hundred years old, and created from it one of
the most seductive coal scuttles in Europe. Everything he does
works. He sets your saw so that it saws. His latches are smooth
and secure. The garden shelter that he founded revolves smoothly
on the ball bearings of a scrapped car and his own iron circle.
Here is a master of his craft indeed! How we all envy him! But
he himself, so perverse is human nature, continually regrets that
he is 'no scholard' and confesses that his ambition was to become
a schoolmaster.

July 1929

Sean Black of Pyecombe   by Ben Darby

Brawny, bearded and in his forties, Sean Black has given new
life to the forge in the Sussex downland village of Pyecombe,
renowned for its shepherds' crooks since the time of Charles II.
They reached their heyday in the last century, when they were
made by the family Mitchell: Charles, who worked till he was

ninety-five, and then his son George, who died in 1956. When Sean Black discovered the forge a year later, it had become a nondescript storehouse; furnace, anvils and even the great bellows were buried.

He became a blacksmith by accident. He is a Scot and started his career by teaching art. When he married, he and his wife went on a long tour in a horse-drawn caravan. Horses have to be shod as well as fed; iron-rimmed wheels have also to be kept in a serviceable state. Sean was forced to do both jobs and liked them. So, when the tour was over, he took a course in agricultural engineering, including smithing, under a Government vocational training scheme in Scotland.

The smithing decided him: that was his life. After a year as journeyman to a Cornish smith, he came to Pyecombe with its crook-making tradition. He could not work there and not make crooks; but there is little demand for them now in the South, so most of his crooks go to shepherds of the Church: bishops carry them in procession, and African bishops have a special liking for them. He also finds that shepherds in his native land like the Pyecombe crook with its longer guide. But his living comes chiefly from his work for architects. He made the candlesticks in St Swithin's chapel over King's Gate at Winchester. He might be asked to design and make a balcony or spiral staircase. He sees iron as a sculptor sees stone.

Summer 1967

Cornish Craftsmen   by Denys Val Baker

A recent survey by the Rural Industries Bureau revealed the existence of four hundred separate crafts in Cornwall. Some of these, such as the painting of sea-shells and the making of jewellery and decorations from pebble-stones, serve the tourist trade, but among them are the traditional country crafts and others which have developed from them.

Archibald Carne, of Truro, is a Cornishman and a countryman. He was born in the later nineties; and, as a youth, he was fascinated by the big steaming horses waiting to be shod in the light of the forge fire, while the smith worked commandingly with the red-hot bars of iron. He would be there whenever school

Francis Cargeeg works in beaten bronze at Hayle. (*Studio St Ives*)

and odd jobs allowed, until, schooldays over, he was apprenticed. His master was an able craftsman and gave him his first instruction in iron and the proper use of tools. At the same time Carne was taking lessons in drawing at Truro Art School, and it has been a combination of the two interests that has made him the master of wrought-iron work.

Francis Cargeeg, also a Cornishman, works a different metal, again with a long tradition. A Celt himself, he became interested in the ancient Celtic craftsmen, whose work in pottery, weaving, enamelling, ecclesiastical stonework and illuminated manuscripts gave to Europe an art of curvilinear and geometric ornament. Some of their greatest achievements were with hammered sheet bronze – that is, copper with a little tin. They obtained astonishing results with it through the technique of embossing designs which we now know as repoussé. These designs were drawn by the flow of light on polished metal, which gave an elusive beauty to what were often flamboyant and bizarre forms. At his workshop in Hayle, Cargeeg works with a very few tools, hammering sheet bronze and beating it into beautifully shaped pots and bowls and shields and trays. His products are useful and decorative, and at the same time works of art, owing to his insistence on making the ornament an integral part of the shape, letting it grow out of it, so that there is an uninterrupted play of light over the surface.

Pottery is another craft particularly associated with Cornwall: a natural enough development in the county which is the home of the china clay industry. Lake's potteries at Truro are famous for their reddish jugs, bowls and pitchers, and there are small potteries at Bodmin, Crowan, Marazion, Newquay and Lamorna. At St Ives, Bernard Leach has his large co-operative pottery, to which students and visitors come from all over the world. It has been working since 1920 and produces not only exquisite works of art, but a large amount of slipware, including soup bowls, casseroles, ramekins, mugs, cups and saucers, plates and teapots. The workers there use the old kick-wheel: as it revolves the potter holds the damp clay between his fingers and slowly shapes it to the required pattern. Attractive designs and decorations are painted on the pots to give them added life and vigour. A form of art at which Bernard Leach and his sons, David and Michael,

Jeanne Stanley works at a rush basket at Grampound in Cornwall.
(*Western Morning News*)

are adepts is 'cutting away' slip coverings to show the contrasting
colours underneath – sgraffito decoration, it is called. Much of
the pottery has the mottled grey colour that so aptly reflects
Cornwall itself.

At Grampound, near Truro, the old Cornish craft of rush
work has been revived by Jeanne Stanley. It began for her one
afternoon when she sat on a stool in a farmyard making a waste-
paper basket out of dried rushes from the borders of the River
Fal. A neighbour stopped to tell her how the old people used to
'traace' the rushes and make them into 'maunds' for field work:
'traacing' was plaiting or tressing the rushes, 'just like 'ee do

Robin Nance (*right*) and his brother, Dicon (*left*) are seen in their St Ives woodware workshop. (*Studio St Ives*)

traace a maid's hair'. In former days the rush workers would take out the pith and rub it in their hands to make wicks for candles and fish-oil lamps. Farmers used rushes to thatch ricks and house-wives made mats from them for their blue-stone floors. Jeanne Stanley has searched into the history of Cornish rush work, dis-covering that there was once a rush factory near Devoran, by Falmouth; that the ancient Britons made rush baskets which were so admired by the Romans that they took them back to Italy; and that at one time Cornish children made their toys out of rushes, tiny baskets being favourites. With all this knowledge as a background, she has steadily developed her art, and her work is now sold all over Britain.

Furniture is being made by Robin and Dicon Nance. Robin Nance attaches great importance to the fact that, as a child, he spent many hours watching a blacksmith at work, thus learning from an early age the everyday nature of all true crafts. He has tried to express this in his furniture, much of which is designed for farmhouses and cottages. He prefers English timbers – oak, walnut, elm, cherry and others – and to use them in the solid, not as veneers. The designs might be described as old-fashioned, but the Nances explain that, in their experience, it is the traditional styles which appeal to country dwellers, and their own familiarity with country ways has undoubtedly influenced their choice.

Wrought iron, hand-beaten copper, pottery, rush work, furniture – these are only five of the crafts of Cornwall. There is also the beautiful hand-printing of Guido Morris, whose posters appear in many places in the county; the embroidery of Erma Harvey-James, who produces appliqué decorations of delicate shades of velvet and silk, interwoven with shining metal threads; the church murals and paintings of Anne Fearon Walke; the sculpture, in Cornish alabaster and granite, of Sven Berlin; the wheelwrights and coopers of Mevagissey, the knitters of Newlyn, the basket-makers of West Penwith, and the old Cornish families which carry on the crafts of smithing, thatching and saddling. In Cornwall life is still a very individual affair, whether it be lived by the members of the 16,000-strong agricultural community or by the fishermen, miners, clay workers or dockers. To that individuality, the craftsmen make an indispensable contribution.

Spring 1951

Basket-making in Wales   by E.M.H.

The basket-maker at the Rural Community Council display of country crafts at the National Eisteddfod sent my mind back to some of the remarkable craftsmen I have met in Welsh country districts and the work they did for the farmers. No farm was complete without a full equipment of 'cewyll', (plural of 'cawell') baskets of various sizes for carrying hay, chaff, and chopped roots from the stack and the barn to the cowhouse and the stable, and most farmers took pride in having good ones. The most usual shape was a kidney-shaped cawell that was slung on the back, and it was a matter of professional pride with the maker that it should, as nearly as possible, hold water. The hay cawell was an open-work affair, with the bottom and the top band closely woven. Mr. John Jones, of Pencarth, Chwilog, in Caernarvonshire, who still practises the old craft, tells me he uses hazel, mountain ash, and willow twigs for this kind of basket. The best baskets are made of hazel. The hazel twigs bend better, and their contraction in drying is more uniform. If mountain ash is used the twigs should be plants of a year's growth. They make a more ornamental basket and worms do not find them palatable,

but they do not dry so satisfactorily as hazel. Willow wands of different colours are used if a pattern is desired, and willow alone is used for flat-bottomed baskets, for all other woods crack if the twigs are bent to make the flat bottom. The disadvantage of willow is that it contracts in drying more than other woods. To-day baskets are less used by farmers, and it is not often now that you find a farmer who can mend his own baskets. That was a common accomplishment thirty years ago. Life on the farm has changed rapidly in recent years. Only the other day Dr Alun Roberts was rejoicing because he had been able to secure a good specimen of the gorse-chopping machine for the museum of agricultural implements he is forming at the University College, Bangor. I was a little startled for, when I was a boy, that machine, now become a museum piece, was to be found, either hand- or water-driven, in every Welsh barn.

October 1932

Coracles on the Teifi   by John Manners

A coracle is a boat lightly constructed of laths of wood with a watertight covering which used to be of animal skin but is now of calico covered in pitch; in other respects, construction has changed very little since prehistoric times. Fishing from coracles now takes place only on the rivers Towy and Teifi in west Wales on a much diminished scale. There is one builder of them on each river, though a handyman could make one without too much difficulty.

On the Teifi John Christmas Thomas, now 70 years of age, is the sole maker. He constructs the frames of split willow laths or more rarely ash and covers them in calico which is finally coated in pitch. The wood is cut in winter in the dormant stage when it has a diameter of $1\frac{1}{2}$in, and is cleft down the middle and shaped to the required dimensions with a thickness of $\frac{1}{4}$in using a draw knife. Nineteen laths are needed, 7ft 6in for longways and 6ft 3in across. Before use they are soaked in water for 24 hours to make them pliable, then interlaced flat on the ground and held in position by stones. The seat of some suitable soft wood with

Willow osiers are still grown along village watersides for the country basket-making workshops. (*Jane Bown*)

The uniquely Welsh craft of coracle building is alive today: Ricky Wilson shows how this smallest of fishing vessels is carried, while Mr Davies of Cenarth demonstrates in an uncovered skeleton how a coracle is paddled with one hand while holding the net with the other. (*John Manners*)

its supports, which also hold the caught fish when the craft is carried slung on the fisherman's back, is placed in position.

Some care is necessary in order that the finished coracle will be balanced correctly. Laths are first threaded through slits that have already been cut in the seat. Starting at the seat a hazel binding consisting of four thin rods is interlaced round the laths which are bent up, and a gunwale is formed as the work proceeds. The frame, which is light and strong, can be made in a day provided everything is prepared beforehand. It is then covered in calico, preferably 72in wide as this does not require any seaming, and the calico is coated with 6lb of pitch mixed with some linseed oil that dries rather like rubber. The finished coracle weighs about 36lb and will stand up to a surprising amount of hard wear, though the skin may need patching occasionally. It is rounded and sloping at one end and almost square at the other to give the necessary stability.

Coracles have only one oar, the upper end of which is rested on the fisherman's shoulder, and the manoeuvering is done with a figure-of-eight movement of the oar blade.

Mr Thomas now makes fifteen to twenty a year, most of them

replacements for the few fishermen still using them and a few for museums. Licences to fish using a pair of coracles and a net are being issued only to existing licence holders, so the number of fishermen will diminish as the present generation retires, a restriction which has led to much local protest.

Coracles are used for catching salmon and more often sea trout called sewin. One of the coracle fishermen is Ricky Wilson of Abercych in Pembrokeshire, who helps work one of the seven pairs still operating on the river in tidal waters between Cilgrennan and the sea where once there were 200 or more of them. He has held a licence for twelve years which allows him to fish at night from 1 March till 30 August except at weekends. With his partner he goes out five nights a week when conditions are right, and being self-employed as a builder can please himself what hours he works.

Coracle fishing is not very lucrative. There is £16 a year for the licence, a new coracle is needed every year at a cost of just over £20, and a replacement net is required from time to time. The catches are far from spectacular. A good night's haul is three salmon trout with a combined weight of 10lb, while the average salmon catch is two a week weighing 10lb each. These are sold for about 50p a lb to a dealer who sells them to Billingsgate, where another dealer sells them to the fishmonger who offers them to the public at £1 a lb. The biggest fish Ricky Wilson has caught weighed 34lb.

The net is a most important piece of equipment. His present ones are home-made of nylon with a weighted rope along the bottom and two ropes at the top. The ropes themselves are unusual, being made out of spun horsehair which stands up to the wet and seemingly lasts for ever. The net is slung under the top rope on horn rings, and when the pull of a fish in the net is felt the second rope is pulled very quickly; the fish is usually enveloped though even the experts have only about 70 per cent success rate. The equipment for closing the net is much the same as for drawing curtains. A curious feature of the gear is the large meshed net which the fish passes through before entangling itself in the smaller one behind, the large meshes making it difficult for the fish to back out providing it is drawn very quickly. The nets must not be more than 20ft wide with a depth of 3ft, and the size of the mesh is governed by regulations. For salmon it is 4in or 6in from knot to knot when stretched.

Coracle fishermen work in pairs with the licence holder on the left and the servant on the right. They drift downstream with the current with the licence holder grasping the tug rope in one hand and operating the one paddle with the other, using his skill to keep the craft heading into the current and at the correct distance from his partner. The hauling in of the net and killing the fish with a wooden truncheon is done by the licence holder.

On reaching the end of the beat the coracles are landed and slung across the back, and the fishermen walk a mile or so up-current and repeat the process some half-dozen times a night. The wind can put a stop to the fishing by making it difficult to row downstream and keep up with the current so that the net is rendered ineffective.

Coracle fishing is more of a sport than a business as the fishermen pit their skill against the fish. The long hours and moderate return are uneconomical in terms of the money that is made, but a few persistent enthusiasts still continue to do it, employing the same methods and equipment that have been used for hundreds and even thousands of years.

Spring 1975

The Broomsquire   by Ernest W. Boxall

My uncle William was one of the last of the Hampshire broomsquires. He lived to be ninety-one and was at work until shortly before his death thirty years ago. I spent nearly all my summer holidays at Hammer Vale, a picturesque hamlet on the borders of Hampshire, Surrey and Sussex, where he had his broom-shops – rough half-open sheds set out on the common. Three other broomsquires also lived in the village at that time.

There were two sorts of brooms – birch and heather. For the first, my uncle would buy the cutting of a small copse, cut the long feathery branches when the catkins were still on them and then store them until the winter. The subsequent trimming was always done by a woman, who was an expert at the job. She worked for hours slicing off the slender branchlets to a length of just over three feet with a sharp curved knife. She measured them with her eye and they never varied by more than an eighth of an inch. When she had cut an armful she would place it in a wooden rest formed by a flat board and two uprights.

Heather was cut towards the end of August, when it was in full bloom. For me that meant a day on Bramshott Common and I usually spent it hunting for mushrooms; the flavour of the heather-grown mushroom is far superior to that of the meadow variety. Dinner was the high spot: sandwiches of home-cured pickled pork between thick slices of new bread, which my grandmother had baked that morning in a wood oven. We drank cold, sweetened tea, untainted with milk. The pinch of green tea which grandmother always put into the pot gave the brew a special flavour. At the end of the day came the ride back home on the top of the bales of heather, tied up with tarry twine and piled high on a wain drawn by two sturdy horses.

Birch and heather brooms were both made by the same method. The broomsquire took a handful of small twigs or sprigs as 'stuffing' and gathered round it his birch or heather. When the bundle was of sufficient thickness he tightened it with a leather thong, and then bound it with two withy bands. These were thin strips of willow cut from the slender uprights that bordered the stream at the bottom of the garden. After they had been dried, they were well soaked for several days in the stream and lifted out only a few hours before they were required. A nick with the broomsquire's knife, and a strip was peeled off in no time.

After the edges had been trimmed with a sharp axe, the brooms were 'handled' with pointed birch or hazel saplings which had been cut in the copse and shaved with a two-handled tool. This exactly fitted the stick, which was held in a primitive wooden vice. Uncle was expert at fitting the handle in the exact centre and prided himself that none of his brooms were lop-sided. The final action was to bore a hole through the bottom of the stick with a large thin-pointed kind of auger and to drive in a wooden peg. The brooms were then fastened up in dozens, thirteen to the dozen being the measure.

Apart from supplies to regular customers the bulk of the sales took place in early spring. Uncle then hired from a local farmer a great wain with a couple of horses and took to the road with a boy of about fourteen to help with them. On several occasions I accompanied him. He would pile the wain high with neatly packed bundles of brooms, which he had little difficulty in selling at stores, stables or country-house gardens. When the stock was almost exhausted he sent a telegram to grandmother, and she despatched a further supply by rail from Liphook. Rail delivery was quick in those days and there were no mistakes. A telegram sent at ten o'clock in the morning brought a new supply within twenty-four hours without fail.

Sometimes we would go through Sussex and even penetrate into Kent as far as Hawkhurst or Cranbrook. At other times we travelled west and reached Winchester or Salisbury. Once we touched the outskirts of London. We would put up at fine old inns, where the food was good, the beds clean and comfortable, and the ale first-class. The journey usually lasted from three to six weeks.

Autumn 1952

The Besomer   by O.A.M.H.

'The besoms I make are good because they're natural', said the old man, as he stood among the ling and young birches. 'Look at them cocoa fibre brooms. Got any strength? How does they wear? 'Course you can make besoms of any kind of branches. Now my father liked wych elm. He'd walk thirty mile a day to get it, pushin' his little barrer, but I'm all fer ling. Know a place where it's as high as me, and tough. And I make whisks o' birch. In the month of May I go to Bewdley Forest and lots of others, but most aren't reg'lar workers like me. They might be pea and potato pickers. Besoms is in my blood; there's been three generations for sure. Began when I was four, mebbe.

'Healthy work, besoming, 'cept in the fall, when the scales from the birch bark make a dust and I cough. It's easy peeling birch in the spring. You take a piece of split oak – I call it a squeezer – and run it along the branches and off comes the bark. Now when it comes to the beginning of fall the bark gets hard and I has to boil the twigs. Ties the twigs in bundles and boils fer eight hours. Boils hard. Must be in rain water, not too fresh but not what stinks.

'Eh, but the whisk trade ain't what is was. Everyone used 'em once; the butcher and the fishmonger had 'em to whisk the flies away. And every pub had its own barm, in wooden pails in a row, and it'd be whisked up to a froth before the women bought their jam pots full, fer their baking. And they'd use the whisks to stir the barm in the breweries. Give it air that way. They'd be called barm sticks. Ain't you never been called barmy? You know, silly, no good, like the froth. Buy a pot of barm and when you get home it's only quarter full. Most of my whisks now goes to the carpet trade to brush away the flights off carpets, you know, the little bits that clings.

'Now mebbe you think besoms is used only for paths but that ain't their chief use. There's a besom man in every ironworks to brush away the hot scales that falls from the chains and wot-nots. And ling don't burn as quick as elm. And when they make anvils there's a man with a besom that picks up water to brush off the scale or they'd be pitted. Why, they'll use half a dozen besoms a day and the men'll not work if there's no besom man, else their shoes'd burn.'

Summer 1942

The Cavern Industry   by John N. Merrill

In the entrance of Peak Cavern, Castleton, Derbyshire, the largest cavern entrance in Britain, stand the rope-walks and wooden machinery that have been used in rope-making for over 400 years. Only in the last year has the industry ceased completely, when Herbert Marrison, the last of a long line of rope-makers, retired in his ninetieth year to Sussex.

All the early travellers to the area visited the cavern mouth and wrote about their findings. Charles Cotton, the renowned friend of Izaak Walton, the fisherman, wrote in his book *The Wonders of the Peak* in 1681 : —

> Now to the cave we come wherein is found
> A new strange thing; a village underground.
> Houses and barns for men and beasts behoof
> With distant walls under one solid roof
> Stacks of hay and turf, which yield a scent.

Inside the cavern next to the rope-walks lived several families engaged in rope-making. They were the Walkers, Dakins, Eyres, Whittinghams and Marrisons. The smoke from the chimneys proved too much for the people working on the rope-walks and eventually the houses were removed, but looking at the cavern roof today you can still see patches of soot from the chimneys.

In the nineteenth century each rope-walk had one family working on it six days a week making all kinds of ropes, such as clothes lines, window sashes, brewers' and hangman's ropes. There was a tradition in the village that each newly-wedded couple received a clothes line as a gift. Being hand-made they lasted for years, often as many as forty. At night the rope-makers made whip-lashes by candlelight.

Herbert Marrison was apprenticed to his father late last century and his apprenticeship lasted three years. He learnt to make loops that never came undone, how to join ropes together, how to make a rope of a specific length without measuring, and just the right amount of twist needed to make a perfect rope. Upon his father's death he carried on his father's wish – 'Don't let the craft die out, lad. Just do a bit now and then – if only a clothes line – to keep it going.' For much of this century he has been the only rope-maker in Castleton. The past custodian of the cavern, Eric Savage, was his helper when needed.

The ropes he made were cheap and long-lasting, which in the long run did not help his business. The newer synthetic fibres and mass-produced ropes began reducing his trade until eventually he was doing it only occasionally. No-one else was interested in the ancient craft, and he was unable to pass on his knowledge of rope-making to anyone. Now that he has retired and left the district his skill has gone with him and the wooden machinery stands idle, as though in a museum.

On each of the five rope-walks can be seen the 'T' posts over which the strands of rope passed, keeping it off the earthen floor. Small wheeled carts upon which the rope stands were secured, and the cart weighted with stones to maintain the right tension, stand close by. Overlooking the stream bed are three twelve-spoked spinning wheels upon which the hemp fibres were spun. On Herbert Marrison's rope-walk is a unique machine for twisting

Entrance to Peak Cavern showing rope-walks and cottage (*Sheffield City Library*)

three rope strands together. A centre geared wheel, turned by hand, operated three equal-spaced small hooked sprockets. To these were attached the individual strands, which passed over the 'T' posts and were secured to the weighted cart. Only by experience could he tell when the right tension had been achieved.

Other Derbyshire villages such as Monyash, Bakewell and Wirksworth had rope-walks and some still retain a street name recording their existence. All ceased towards the end of the nineteenth century. In the late 1930s the last rope-maker of Tansley, John Barber, ceased work. His grandfather had started the business in 1810 and the rope was made on similar lines to that at Castleton. To prove his dexterity he often made ropes blindfolded. In 1932 when aged seventy he commented, 'In the old days we did a tremendous lot of work for all the mills in the district, but today most of our work comes from farmers, who want halter and waggon ropes that will stand up to work and last.' Like the horses, the old village craft has gone in Derbyshire, and the wooden items in Peak Cavern and the occasional street named Ropewalk are our only reminders of this fascinating craft.

Summer 1976

G. Elliott, Saddler by John Saunders

A little stone cottage juts out from a row of three at one end of the village of North Newington in Oxfordshire. In its front window, square-paned and painted white, hang bits of curb-chains, stirrup-irons and leathers, riding switches and halters. Outside and below the window, on an iron railing which barely separates the cottage from the curving street, rests a row of saddles. Above is a board with bold white letters on a black ground: 'G. Elliott. Saddler, Etc.'

The side door was open, and through it I saw George Elliott himself seated at his bench, saddle on knee and tools laid out before him. At first I wondered that he could work there at all, for the shop was no more than eight feet across and so full of goods and gear that he looked to be a permanent fixture, hemmed in comfortably and unable to stir from his seat. Boxes, drawers and tins rose beside him; bales of wool and hides were stacked behind. From floor to ceiling, as on the wall outside, there hung bags and bridles, riding crops and thongs, tail-cases, reins and harness of all kinds. Even a sporting print or two had found space among the orderly confusion.

George Elliott rose to greet me and soon explained that he is a fixture only in the sense that he has carried on his trade in North Newington for a very long time. A man of sixty-six who looks ten years younger, he was apprenticed as a boy to a saddler at Moreton-in-Marsh. He had been lame since the age of five, so he had to have a sedentary occupation. After two or three years as a journeyman with a harness-maker in Banbury, he set up on his own. 'Nearly all cart-horse collars it was in those days', he told me. 'I must have made hundreds of them. And you could reline and stuff a collar for two and ninepence; now it would cost you three pounds.'

Gradually the business dwindled, and he had to turn to making handbags, dog collars and leads, and so on. During the last war he sent scores of pairs of sandals all over the world. Trade has picked up a bit in recent years, for his is a hunting district and there is a riding school near by; children seem to take up pony-riding more and more. Now the only working saddler in north Oxfordshire, he gets orders from miles around. 'I'm often sitting here till half-past eight or nine in the evening', he said. 'Being on my own, I have to get through the work somehow.'

Winter 1958

Racing Saddles   by C. F. Snow

It takes a skilled saddler at least three days of hard work to complete a racing saddle such as Stan Ward of East Ilsley, Berkshire, makes. These saddles weigh only three to five pounds but have to stand hard wear. They are made of pigskin, the best being cut from the middle of the skin where the leather is of the finest quality. Each is made to fit a particular horse and, to get the exact measurements, the saddler uses a thin lead pipe which he can bend easily to the required size. After stitching and lining the saddle, he stuffs it with best quality lambs' wool, which is soft but resilient, and absorbent. An experienced craftsman can judge just the right amount of stuffing and ensure its even distribution to provide a clear channel for a current of cool air along the horse's back. The finished saddle is lined with top-grade doeskin and quilted with satin, all by hand.

The three-hundred-year-old shop where Stan Ward works was once the saddler's shop of a large estate. Behind it is the stone block with iron ring where old horses were slaughtered in days when many saddlers prepared and tanned the skins they needed. The workrooms behind and over the shop are packed with leather, saddles, bridles, whips, horse-rugs, all kinds of harness and a vast assortment of tools: awls, leather prickers, punches, needles and countless others. Stan Ward still repairs an occasional collar or piece of harness for a farmer; but he is kept working at full capacity, twelve hours a day, making saddles for racehorses, hunters, hacks and ponies, and repairing old ones.

Summer 1963

The Snob and his Butts   by M. A. Wilson

No one called him a cobbler – it was a description which he intensely disliked. 'I make boots and shoes' he used to say, 'and I mend them as good as new.' (This was not quite true but I never dared tell him so!) 'You can call me a snob (an old term for a shoemaker) but never call me a cobbler. I am one of St Crispin's men, the patron saint of shoemakers.'

It is many years since I used to go into the little front room of his cottage and watch him at his work. He would sit on a stool at a low bench below the window facing the village street. A customer had to push open the top part of the door and then from the inside unlatch the lower part. The floor was littered with boots, shoes, leather, shavings, trimmings, paper, old nails, dust and dirt. In the summer this was occasionally swept into one corner awaiting the colder weather, when it was dumped in an old Tortoise stove, which emitted very little heat, a lot of smoke, and a lot more smell.

He was very strong of arm and shoulder, but crippled, and in those days there were not many trades in a country district for a cripple. He was dedicated to his job, and quite convinced that no one else used such good materials. These were bought from a currier whose traveller called every two months, when an order was placed and the previous purchases paid for. For this purpose the shoemaker would reach down from a shelf a round tin which contained half-crowns. Every time a half-crown was paid to him he put it in this tin, and as he said 'When the traveller comes there's not much more money needs finding.'

His order to the traveller was full of strange words: butts (the full hide suitable for sole leather), bends (half a butt), bellies (the underneath of a hide suitable for non-wearing purposes), kip (waterproof upper leather for heavy boots), willow (a soft upper leather for lighter boots and shoes), tingles (sharp nails for soling), hobs (heavy round nails for farm boots), fitters (heavy square nails, shaped to fit when nailed around toes and heels), rivets (nails for soling), quick black (a liquid used preparatory to putting on edging waxes), hemp (thin rough thread, multiplied and waxed to make a 'thread'), bristles (from hogs' backs, fitting to the end of a 'thread'), and drag knives (a blade right-angled to the shaft, for cutting towards one; a safety knife).

He had many trade tricks and peculiarities, such as making sole patterns by placing a piece of newspaper on the sole of the shoe and rasping round it; hammering the leather on an old flat iron held between his knees, gently at first, then harder and harder; running his thumb nail around leather soles to mark an edge for cutting 'the channel' for sewing; honing his knife blade on the back hairs of his head; licking a blade before cutting rubber; and tasting the cut edge of a new piece of leather and leaving a certain amount of saliva on it 'to see how it takes the water'.

He died in his seventies, at his bench, quietly sitting there with some completed work in his lap. It was said he had an enlarged heart through lack of exercise. He was a non-smoker and non-drinker, thrifty and an ardent chapel attender. An orphan and a Cottage Homes boy, he left his savings of nearly £600 to the couple with whom he lodged. No one took over his business. His goods and the tools he so loved and treasured were all sold to a junk man.

Summer 1973

Cobbler, Mend My Shoe   by Eric Powell

At the turn of the century my father kept a small shop offering boots and shoes of the tough practical types essential for the rough hilly country round the village of Blakeney in the Dean Forest. Behind was the workshop with a pile of leather hides known as 'sides' in one corner, and a quantity of box calf, chrome, *glacé* kid and patent leathers for making and repairing uppers.

It took Father half a day to make a pair of boots or shoes. He had a reputation for good workmanship, and orders for boots to measure came from far outside the village. A pair of farm worker's or miner's boots cost nine shillings with a perfect fit guaranteed; more fashionable footwear cost twelve and six. He would also take on any kind of leather repairs from gloves to harness, as there was no saddler in the village. Many of his customers were school-children, who might have to walk up to seven miles to school over rough stony roads. But if shoes caked with mud were brought in for repair, the customer was handed a scraper and told to clean them up outside.

All the machinery was operated by hand or foot. The heavy press for cutting out soles had an enormous fly-wheel; when this was revolving at speed I would stand on the foot-pedal and have a bouncing ride for about half a minute. At the back of the large work-bench were boxes of rivets and nails. Father would stand behind the last with the boot or shoe held firmly in position on it by a looped rope, the lower end pulled tight by his foot. With a strip of steel in his right hand, he would fish out a quantity of rivets or nails with the left, blow on them to remove the dust and pop them into his mouth. Taking them out one at a time, he would place them where required and hammer them home with the speed and exactness of a machine. I never saw him miss the target or hit his fingers.

When I got home from school I often helped Father with finishing off the soles, rasping the edges, smoothing off with emery paper, applying wax and rubbing them round with a burnishing tool warmed on a small oil heater. He made his own wax. Pitch was the main ingredient, but when the warm mixture was being kneaded and stretched in his hands it looked like dark molten toffee.

Another of my jobs was to make the strong waxed thread for sole-stitching. It was quite an art to hold several strands of white hemp of the desired length in the left hand and twist them between warmed wax with the other. The thread was then stretched, and finally Father rolled it repeatedly over the leather apron on his thigh. I believe some of our old apprentices still make their own thread.

Father was a good salesman. I remember one well-to-do lady coming for a pair of walking boots. After trying on everything of her size in the shop she was not satisfied; she supposed she would have to make a tiring journey into Gloucester to find a pair of the right quality. 'Just a minute,' said Father, 'I think I have the very thing you want upstairs'. Gathering up the scattered boots, he disappeared and returned shortly with a pair which he assured her was 'the very best in the shop. You won't get better anywhere'. The price he mentioned was half a crown higher than any of the others, but these were a perfect fit. 'I'll take them', said the lady. 'Why on earth didn't you show me them before?' After she had gone Father turned to me: 'Same pair as she liked in the first place, but thought too cheap', he said. 'She'd have had to pay more in Gloucester for worse boots, not to mention the travelling.'

Winter 1969

A Country Tailor Looks Back   by Hugh Abercrombie

It was at the turn of the century that I started to serve my five-year apprenticeship to a country tailor. He lived in the rich farming district of the Lancashire Fylde – a countryside stretching green and fresh, as yet unspoilt, between the estuaries of Wyre and Ribble. The shop, house and workrooms have remained virtually unchanged in the ownership of one family for four tailoring generations although, when the business was started by John Fisher at St Michael's-on-Wyre in 1835, the shop was elsewhere in the village. The workroom, situated over the stables at the back of the house and lit by roof-lights and windows along one wall, is still reached by the time-honoured method of loft-ladder and trapdoor. And the good work still goes on there – work of great variety not only for local country gentlemen, farmers and gamekeepers, but also for wealthy customers in the coastal resorts round Morecambe Bay and throughout the Lake District. Most country tailors and outfitters made only to measure, as we did; so there were no stocks left over and going to waste.

The youngest of five apprentices, I began work at a quarter to six, summer and winter, when I had to fill and light the large ceiling-lamp which was our only illumination until daylight came. I then lit the stove, which contained an interior compartment with a door like an oven so that the fire burned under it and up the sides; into this I put the heavy tailoring irons weighing from 16 to 18lb. each. Three-quarters of an hour was required to heat a very heavy iron, but it stayed hot for an hour. The five tailors arrived at six o'clock, and a girl machinist at seven. There was no such thing as being late; it was unheard of. Work continued steadily until eight and, after half-an-hour for breakfast, until noon. We had an hour for dinner and worked through from one to six without a tea-break. The hours totalled fifty-eight and a half a week.

Under the large oil lamp which hung from the rafters was a dais or platform raised about a foot off the ground; and on this we all sat cross-legged in a circle directly beneath the light. The practice of tailors in sitting cross-legged over their work began in the early days when everything was made by hand. The cloth rested across the worker's knees, and all his accessories and

The workshop where tailor Hugh Abercrombie started his apprentice-ship at the turn of the century was almost unchanged when pictured in 1967. (*E. Abercrombie*)

trimmings were spread around him, so that he did not have to waste time by getting up to look for something. The pressing of garments was likewise done cross-legged on a sleeve-board across the knees. This manner of sitting could be very painful for a newcomer to the trade; but after a few months he would stay that way all day without discomfort.

The shop's crew consisted of Elijah Barton, the leader and a highly-skilled coat-maker – he could complete a gentleman's jacket in a day, a good proportion of it hand-sewn – Harry Hodgson, Joe Iddon, Joe Haslem, Old Sam and myself. Sam was a specialist in ladies' corsets – stiff terrifying garments which looked like armour-plate after he had finished with them and must have been very tight under the arms. We had a surprising variety of work: gamekeepers' coats, morning coats with bound edges, riding breeches with buckskin strappings and box-cloth leggings, plenty of whole-fall and split-fall trousers, also the new fly-front trousers then coming into vogue and an endless number of waist-coats, double-breasted and with collars. After five years I was able to make anything that was wanted.

The head of the firm, John Fisher (son of John Fisher the

founder), was then in middle life. He had three sons, Septimus, Charlie and Percy. All helped with the cutting out of garments, and Percy used to take the horse and trap round the countryside for orders, visiting farms and country houses with his pattern books and rolls of cloth. Measurements were taken and cloth selected, then back to the workroom for the cutting out and making up; off again a week later for fitting, and the following week with the finished garment – and perhaps to book further orders on the way. This manner of business is still carried on by the family, though the horse and trap have been replaced by the motor car and the field of endeavour has considerably widened.

The business was noted for great skill in cutting breeches, mostly in heavy strong tweed known as Bliss's tweed, woven in Oxfordshire. Perhaps the most tedious job was the making of a gamekeeper's coat with its nine pockets – four outside, and on the inside two hare pockets, two breast pockets and a ticket pocket – and gun-pads on the shoulders. We took about two and a half days to make one of these coats, more than a full day's work going into the pockets alone.

During the summer we were usually visited by one or two tramp tailors – skilled coat-makers who seemed unable to settle anywhere for long at a time. They would come into the shop, broke to the world, get a shilling or two to pay for a night's lodging in the village, stay on for a job of work and, after two or three weeks, push off again along the road. They tramped on to the nearest town, which might be Lancaster, Blackburn or Preston, and so back to our country shop 'round the rink' as they termed it. Each had his own 'rink' or beat, and in winter they seemed to reside in the workhouse.

In those days a fully experienced country tailor was paid 24s a week, and a girl machinist about 18s; an apprentice received only 10s for board, lodging and washing. I used to get a free haircut thrown in, because my landlady, a grand countrywoman, cut my hair for me. I always recall her advice when my time came to leave the village: 'When seeking lodgings, look out for a fat landlady and a fat cat, and you will be well looked after'.

Our only holidays consisted of a few days off at Christmas and the three bank holidays. No holidays with pay! As an apprentice I used to spend Whit Monday whitewashing the workroom, for which I received a shilling. There was no dole, state welfare or national insurance, of course, but John Fisher put away 2s a week for each apprentice, to be drawn now and again for such items as clothes and shoes. A new pair of boots cost 8s, a shirt about 2s. He gave me one suit, and my landlady used to knit socks for me. A suit would cost about 35s, a gamekeeper's coat about 30s.

The village also had a sick benefit society, and into this fund John Fisher paid 10s a year, so that if anyone was ill, on presentation of a doctor's certificate, the man would receive 10s a week for thirteen weeks; out of this would come payment for medicines and so on. But the village people were a healthy lot, living on wholesome country food, without money to spare for smoking and drinking, or time for boredom to prey on the nerves. In fact, no member of the workroom staff was away ill all the time I was there. Such complaints as neurosis, stomach ulcers and thrombosis were unheard of. We were there to work, and we worked as fast as we could consistently with skilled and good craftsmanship: and as we worked Elijah Barton, who had a fine tenor voice, would sing us the old Lancashire folk songs.

Now they have music of another kind 'while they work', and electricity to provide all the power and light required. There are no longer tailors on the staff; the whole of the work goes through the capable hands of girls at long tables. 'If you wanted a tailor,' Harry Hodgson told me on a recent visit to the old haunts, 'you would have to dig one up out of the cemetery'.

Backed by so long and honourable a tradition of service and craftsmanship, and with as much work in hand as the staff can handle, there has been no need for a shop window; in fact, it is something of an anachronism. But on my visit the window contained, among other things, a small item that set a startling contrast between the old and the new: 1900, Bliss's tweed at 6s a yard, and now, 1967, Tibetan goat's-hair cloth (in black and fawn, soft and light as silk) at £35 a yard, putting the cost of a coat at about £175. The villagers pass by with a smile.

Of the workroom staff of my apprentice days only two remain: Harry Hodgson, aged eighty-eight and still living in the village, and myself, eighty-four. After a lifetime as a master tailor and cutter I still keep the irons hot and thread in the needle. Boredom and retirement are not for me.

Summer 1967

Rain or Shine   **by W. Hamond**

Our friend Mr Norton of the general stores accepted a bundle of broken umbrellas with his usual nonchalance and instructed the customer to call for them at the end of the week. Knowing him to be a surprisingly versatile man, I inquired whether he would mend them himself.

'Why yes, sir', he assured me, 'my old father used to make 'em, and we used to help him when we was kids. Them big old gig umbrellas was always wanted, and that was Father's trade. He used to buy the whalebone cut to length – they was all whalebone

Tom Allan of Cloughton, near Scarborough, pictured in 1960, when he claimed to be the oldest working tailor in Britain. Born in 1863, he made hundreds of suits costing from £2 to £3, often on twelve months credit for farmworkers who were paid annually at Martinmas. Children stopped on their way to school to watch him at work. (*J. F. Seaman*)

them days – but it had to be split; and it would split too, beautiful. Then us kids 'ud get to work on it, fining it down to the proper size. Seven or eight years old I was then, and we got twopence a dozen for making the ribs. We had a little flat piece of iron with a hole in it, and the ribs had to go through the hole, not too tight and not too loose or they wouldn't fit the joints. We had what they call a thumb-plane to shave the whalebone down with, and there was a jig for to fit the ribs into, to get 'em together. Only thing with whalebone, though, is the mice. Ah, mice do always come after whalebone. 'Tis all right till you split it, but then there's a kind of fishy smell. We had traps set all over the place, but you never could get rid of 'em proper nor keep 'em away.

'Then there was ordinary umbrellas, of course, but they was green silk in them days and all lined; the ladies would have 'em silk-lined in all fancy colours. And then there was the parasols. The ladies was crazy on parasols sixty year ago. Dozens they would have. The Earl's ladies 'ud get the latest fashion books from London with all the new styles in, and then Father 'ud get orders to make 'em up. Beautiful they was, every colour you could think of, and all lace and ribbons and bows and fringe. Then every one must have a gold band with a coat of arms on. After that the great long handles come in, shaped like a shepherd's crook. Four foot long or more they was; 'twas the fashion, see? The ladies would have 'em, and perfect they had to be, too.

'How big do you think the largest gig umbrella was my father ever made? Seven foot across. 'Twas for a farmer as lived hereabouts, and when he put that up it sheltered all them as was riding with him and pretty near covered the horse as well. Forty-five shilling that cost, a good price in them days, but that was a special order. Ah, and with all us kids to help; Father couldn't ha' done it without that.

'Do you know, sir? A lady come in not long ago with an umbrella, broke a rib of it she had, accidental; and darn me if 'twasn't one my old father made fifty years ago. Been in her family all them years. Green silk it was with a pink silk lining good as the day it was made. Colour wasn't even faded. Ah, they made things to last in them days'.

Winter 1959